CELEBRATE
YOUR
CHILD
THE ART OF
HAPPY
PARENTING

Richard **C**arlson, Ph.D.

N E W   W O R L D   L I B R A R Y

© 1992 Richard Carlson, Ph.D.

Published by New World Library
58 Paul Drive
San Rafael, California 94903

Cover Design: Joe Fay
Text Design & Typography: TBH/Typecast, Inc.
Word Processing: Deborah Eaglebarger

Library of Congress Cataloging-In-Publication Data
Carlson, Richard, 1961-
   Celebrate your child : the art of happy parenting / Richard Carlson.
      p.   cm.
   ISBN 1-880032-08-2 (alk. paper)
   1. Parenting—United States. 2. Happiness in children—United States. 3. Parent and child—United States. I. Title
HQ755.8.C38 1992
649'.1—dc20   92-12116
                                                                  CIP

ISBN 1-880032-08-2
First Printing, October 1992
Printed in the U.S.A. on acid-free paper

10   9   8   7   6   5   4   3   2   1

To Kristine

*My partner in parenting—
my partner in life.*

I love you!

CONTENTS

INTRODUCTION

Portrait of a Happy Child　　ix

CHAPTER ONE

The Art of Happy Parenting　　1

CHAPTER TWO

Self-Esteem: The Foundation of Happiness　　7

CHAPTER THREE

Encouraging Inner-Directedness　　11

CHAPTER FOUR

Living in the Present　　19

CHAPTER FIVE

Eliminating Hurry　　23

CONTENTS

CHAPTER SIX

Quiet Time   31

CHAPTER SEVEN

Children and Moods   37

CHAPTER EIGHT

Judgment-Free Activity   49

CHAPTER NINE

Looking for the Good   55

CHAPTER TEN

Avoiding Criticism   69

CHAPTER ELEVEN

Taking Risks   75

CHAPTER TWELVE

Boredom   83

CHAPTER THIRTEEN

Cultivating a Grateful Attitude   93

PORTRAIT OF A HAPPY CHILD

DOES THIS SOUND FAMILIAR?

It's Friday evening and you've just finished another week at work. Life seems frantic. The bills need to be paid, dinner needs to be cooked, the phone is ringing, people are asking you for favors, you have calls to return, and now the sink is leaking. What next?

You have to go the grocery store and bring your youngster along. You love him, but you know that he is likely to throw a fit in the store. He's always difficult around this time of day—restless, fidgety, bored, frustrated. It seems he can never just sit still or think of ways to entertain himself—especially in public. He doesn't seem all that happy.

DOES THIS SOUND BETTER?

It's Friday evening and you've just finished another week at work. Life seems frantic. The bills need to be paid, dinner needs to be cooked, the phone is ringing, people are asking you for favors, you have calls to return, and now the sink is leaking. What next?

You will go to the grocery store and bring your youngster. He's a joy to be around, and helps take your mind off your concerns because he's fun, creative, and calm. He's adaptable and easygoing, and finds the simplest things enjoyable. He makes light of problems and sees the best in every situation. It's reassuring to be with him because it reminds you that all your hard work is worth it. You always learn something new from him and, in fact, you often find yourself wishing you were more like him. You know in your heart that he's a happy child.

Promote Positive Change

If this second scenario appeals to you more than the first, this book is for you. Happy children are a delight to be around. They emanate joy everywhere they go. Happy children believe that life is an exciting adventure to be lived moment by moment; they are self-reliant, inner-directed, innovative thinkers—future leaders of the world. They are willing to try just about anything, meet people, explore the unknown. Happy children are not afraid of failure, and when they do fail, they pick themselves up and start all over. Happy children are creative. They are willing to try different ways of doing things and change habits when it's appropriate. Happy children love education in the same way that they love life. They love to learn, to try, and to invent. Happy children are loving, compassionate, friendly, and helpful. Happy children love their family and friends, and they love being part of the human family.

This book will promote positive changes in your children. Everything you learn from this book is geared toward having your children think more positively about themselves, which in turn will enable them to have a more complete and positive self-image.

We all gravitate toward what we think about most. If we think too much about those things we don't want in our life, we find ourselves surrounded by those very things—because our minds move toward, not away from, what we think about.

After incorporating some of the ideas here, your children will, among other things, be more likely to:

Use their imaginations

Think positively about themselves

Be less critical of themselves and others

Eliminate the word "boredom" from their vocabulary

Think of new and creative ways to spend their time

Do nice things for others—including you

Develop new interests and skills

Have an all-around more positive attitude

Feel better about themselves and probably about you, too

The Origin of Happiness

Runners take your mark. Get set. . . . Go! Happiness is much like a group of runners waiting for the starting gun to begin a race. It's an explosion waiting to happen. It helps to understand the origin of happiness if you want to raise happy children. Conversely, if you understand where it doesn't come from, you can learn to avoid actions that take your children away from happiness.

The origin, or underlying principle, of raising happy children is simple but profound: *Happiness is inherent in every human being.* We all begin life with a clean slate: pure, sweet, free, and happy. If you watch a room full of young children you will see that what I am saying is true. Each child is unique, naturally proud, and satisfied with life. When the adventure of life begins, all kids are curious, self-loving, adventuresome, spontaneous, special, awestruck, and filled with love.

All children have their own way of being in the world, with unique talents to pursue and special gifts to offer, but in this fundamental sense they are all the same. Our job as parents, though often difficult, is straightforward: to prevent this inherent happiness from slipping away. If you understand this principle—that happiness is inherent in every human being—and you strive to make parental decisions that support this principle, you will be on the path to raising a happy child. It may not always be easy, but it is that simple. Everything you say and do as a parent will either support, or go against, this basic concept.

The purpose of this book is to reveal to you the real-life actions and habits that foster happiness. You will become more aware of the negative messages you might be giving your children that can be cleverly disguised as "loving," as well as learning alternative communication that will foster their inherent happiness.

Happiness comes from the process of allowing that which is already inside your child to develop. Just as seeds will grow into flowers given the right environment, so will children maintain their happiness if they are encouraged and provided with a fertile environment for its growth.

Raising a happy child is one of the most rewarding things you can achieve as a human being, but it can take enormous patience and persistence. In many ways it is easier to squelch the inherent happiness right out of your kids, to make them conform, to listen and not be heard, to force them to do as they are told, to be like everyone else. But in the long run, you'll be glad if you don't take that route. Encouraging your child to be like everyone else crushes his or her own uniqueness; never taking risks can squeeze the fun and excitement out of life, and being a conformist can drive your child to depend on outward approval to generate self-respect.

I have no doubt that you will see the truth in what you are about to read. The tricky part will be implementing these ideas into your daily life as a parent. As you read, imagine how grateful your children will be when they grow up and have children of their own. Imagine what it will be like to hear the following from your grown-up child: "Thanks Mom (or Dad) for allowing me to be me. Thanks for allowing me to express myself and to live my life based on my dreams. I consider you the truest and dearest of friends because people who truly care want their friends to be themselves, not clones of others. Thank you for having so much patience with me, and for putting up with me during those times when I was difficult and stubborn, when I had to do things my own way even though you didn't think it was in my best interest—or yours. Thank you for respecting me enough to let me live my own life. I love you and I will never forget you."

Whether or not you ever get such a welcome "thank you," you will know that you did everything you could to allow your child to be as free and happy as possible.

—*Richard Carlson, Ph.D.*
Walnut Creek, California

CHAPTER ONE

THE ART
OF HAPPY
PARENTING

Children are natural mimics who act like their parents
in spite of every attempt to teach them good manners.

—ANONYMOUS

MAHATMA GANDHI, THE GREAT Indian political and spiritual leader, was quoted as saying, "My life is my message." Perhaps this is never more true than in the field of parenting. Although each child is unique and special, and fully capable of genuine happiness, each will learn the basics of life from his parents. Your children will look to you to teach them about life. They will observe how you respond to adversity, disappointment, success, and failure, and model themselves after your example. Your children will tune their antennae in your direction when others criticize you; they will want to find out the "appropriate" response to criticism—how should they feel and how should they act? They will watch to see how important approval from others is to you, how much emphasis should be placed on the future or the past, and whether they should be "inner-directed" or externally motivated.

Your children will look to you to discover the meaning of

life, to find out what's important and what's not. They learn from you when it's appropriate to express anger, frustration, and irritation. They will wonder how you feel about yourself and about living, how grateful or apathetic you are for the gift of life. Your children will want to know, "Just how good about myself can I feel?" They will ask themselves (consciously or unconsciously) questions like, "What are my limitations, my drawbacks, my strengths, my weaknesses?" They will ponder: "Is the world a happy place? Do I deserve to be happy? Am I happy? Is it possible to be happy?" They will eventually wonder why most people don't remain happy, and they may even spend quite a bit of time wondering why you don't seem happy.

Parenting is the most wonderful and challenging "job" you will ever have in your life. If you think about it, the responsibility is awesome. We are going to try to raise happy children—and yet how many of us have learned to be happy ourselves? How do we bring out genuine happiness in our children if we haven't mastered this ourselves? After all, children are little mimics. We can preach and lecture all we want, but to our children, our life really is our message. Our "way of being" in the world, our mannerisms, our reactions, our patience (and lack of it), what we say, what we do, how we spend our time, and how we respond to various situations, will ultimately determine our children's "operating manual" for life.

I can offer no fancy theories or sophisticated parenting techniques. Instead I will share my own commonsense approach to raising happy children, based on my own experience of being a happy person and being around other happy parents and their happy children. I will, in fact, stay away from theory and focus more on the practical. I want every parent, or future parent, who reads this book to be able to see the simple logic in what I have written—and I want everyone to be able to implement the information immediately. All of this applies equally to parents with children of any age, even grown children. In other words, it applies to all of us.

Although I consider myself a very "good" parent, I do not consider myself an "expert." I'm not convinced there is such a thing as an expert parent. What I can say is that I have two beautiful children whom I love as much as anything in life. I have always loved children, and for more than a decade now, I have been working with children and their parents. I have been a big brother for Big Brothers of America, and have worked for Child Assault Prevention teaching children how to protect themselves. I am also a professional bodyworker, whose goal is to help children retain a positive outlook about their own bodies and self-image, and I maintain an ongoing Stress Management practice in which I work with children and teenagers (and their parents) teaching them to be happier.

Your Children Look to You

The most consistent observation I have made over the years is that all children tend to mimic their parents—the good, the bad, and the indifferent. Most children base most of their impressions, their assumptions, and their reactions to life on their parents' overall vision of life. I have concluded from my observations that if parents set a happier, more conscious, and consistently loving and grateful example, their children will be far more likely to retain the wonderful qualities they were born with.

I am not the first parent to come to these somewhat obvious conclusions. But if the conclusions are so obvious, then why on earth are there so many unhappy children? The answer appears to be our own lack of awareness as parents of the "hidden messages" we give our children which come from our own way of being: the way we react to life. Children see everything we do as appropriate. If we argue, arguing becomes appropriate; if we seek approval, seeking approval becomes appropriate; if we put ourselves down, then putting oneself down becomes appropriate. What I have learned is that no theories of parenting will create happy children unless there is conscious parental involvement. And, parental involvement, in the sense I am referring to, is a commitment to personal happiness and a commitment to setting an example as a happy, contented person. Without you as the example, no amount of lecturing, theory, or parenting skills will bring forth lasting happiness in your children.

Parents who are acutely aware of how important their example is to their children are almost always able to achieve greater patience, perspective, wisdom, and happiness themselves. In this respect, parenting can be looked at as a wonderful opportunity to become a happier person yourself! The focus of this book is to help you give your children positive, life-affirming messages that will become their way of seeing and thinking about life.

Parents who turn their energy toward raising happy children quickly discover an encouraging phenomenon. Everything else seems to work itself out. That's right, everything! Children who are happy have a natural sense of curiosity and a passion for learning. They love to excel in virtually everything they do and are equally capable of doing things

4

"just for the fun of it." Happy children are kind, caring, passionate, and loving people. Parents discover that good behavior, high performance, manners, and a thirst for education all develop in a healthy way when their children are happy. So rather than struggle individually with providing a good education, teaching morals, and the behaviors of day-to-day living, strive to reach one fundamental goal—genuine and lasting happiness. Everything good that follows is a natural extension of this fundamental state of mind.

CHAPTER TWO

SELF-ESTEEM: THE FOUNDATION OF HAPPINESS

This above all: to thine own self be true.

—SHAKESPEARE, *HAMLET*

T O A LARGE DEGREE, ONGOING, genuine happiness stems from a strong sense of self-esteem—a feeling of self-assurance, a quiet knowing that all the answers you need are available within yourself. Without a strong and genuine sense of self-esteem, a person is left with a feeling of anxiety, of overcautiousness and irritation. There might also be a feeling of insecurity, boredom, and a lack of confidence, the feeling that someone else should provide you with the answers you need.

We have all met, or at least seen, children who demonstrate a shining sense of self-esteem—children who feel great about themselves, who aren't overly concerned with what others think about them, who demonstrate a charismatic quality of self-worth. These children—who, deep down, feel good about themselves—are truly happy. Very simply, these children feel they can afford to be happy. They don't worry like other children might and they don't seek unnecessary approval.

As parents, we know intuitively that our children are born with a strong sense of self-esteem. Just spend a small amount of time with young children playing, and you realize that all children naturally feel good about their own efforts. They don't worry about how they're doing, and constantly evaluate their performances; instead, children focus only on the task at hand and have a great time doing it. Even when children get frustrated, they quickly forget their irritation, learn from their mistakes, and move on to the next activity and more enjoyment.

Where Does It Go?

As we move out of childhood, we may appear to lose our self-esteem, but it is never completely lost. It is only covered up by negative, insecure thoughts that we have come to believe are true. "I'm not doing well enough" or "I'm always bored" or "I can't do it" or "I'm stupid." These thoughts and others like them, if left unchecked, will eventually dominate the way we see ourselves. And the way we view ourselves will determine how we feel and behave.

Deep within all children, the inherent feeling of self-esteem remains. There has never been, nor will there ever be, a child who doesn't have this potential to feel good, because in the absence of learned negative thoughts, children are left with their original feeling of self-esteem. Children labeled "unhappy" have been discovered laughing and smiling when they are left alone. During those moments they are forgetting, at least temporarily, the negative thoughts that lowered their spirits. Without reminders to be "an unhappy child" the opportunity exists for negative thoughts to disappear and a more positive feeling to surface. It is our job to help our children let go of the negative thoughts and beliefs they have about themselves, and help them to regain positive feelings. Teach them that any thoughts they have about themselves that don't feel good aren't worth believing. Their negative thoughts don't have to be taken so seriously; they can choose which thoughts to believe and which ones to ignore. We can teach our children to be the masters of their own lives by believing in themselves and their abilities.

Children are like little sponges. They soak up the words and actions of their parents' classmates, friends, siblings, and other role models, more than we imagine. Innocent little negative comments from friends, or even from strangers, register somewhere in their brains—and stay there in the form of a memory. As more and more self-defeating thoughts get stored in memory, he or she begins to think in those terms.

A child's memory is a storage vault for information—a computer which stores data about the world and about himself. When a little boy's computer is filled with negative information, he will think about himself in a negative light. The more that information is reinforced, the more ingrained it becomes in his thinking.

Bringing Back Self-Esteem

The good news is that self-esteem, the foundation of happiness and creativity, is relatively easy to get back. Because self-esteem is natural to us, we need only learn to ignore any thoughts that interfere. Replace the negative thoughts we have about ourselves with positive ones.

There is really nothing that holds a fearful or negative image in place other than our own thinking. There was a time, for example when we were kids ourselves, when many of us believed there was a "big-foot" monster, or similar beast, living in our closet. Despite our parents' reassurances to the contrary, we went on believing that the monster did, in fact, exist.

At some point, however, we realized the monster wasn't real, except in our own imaginations. Once we were convinced of this, we were never again frightened by the monster.

We have all probably developed our own version of the big-foot monster who lives to attack our well-being and self-esteem—destroying our happiness. So rather than feeling good about ourselves and our efforts, as we once did, instead we use our own imaginations against ourselves and come up with thoughts such as, "I'll never be able to learn this skill," "I can't think of anything useful to do," and so forth.

But these are still only thoughts. Just as we stopped believing in our thoughts of the closet monster, we can also stop paying so much attention to thoughts about our shortcomings and faults. We can (and must) teach our children to do the same.

For a child to live up to his greatest potential, it is critical to have a strong sense of self-esteem. So it is important that we as parents do everything possible to provide an environment that fosters the most happiness and creative growth.

Plant the seeds of happiness in your children. Learn what you can do, and should not do, to put the odds in your child's favor to live the happiest life possible. All children have the potential for happiness and creative genius; we must permit our children to actualize this potential.

CHAPTER THREE

ENCOURAGING INNER-DIRECTEDNESS

Just trust yourself, then you will know how to live.

—GOETHE, *FAUST*

TO BE "INNER-DIRECTED" means to turn within yourself to find the answers you are looking for. Children who are inner-directed do just that. They trust their own intuition, instincts, and creativity over anyone else's opinion, and learn to make wise "age-appropriate" decisions for themselves. Ideally, this becomes a healthy lifetime pattern.

Inner-directed children grow up to be self-reliant, confident, productive adults who take personal responsibility for their actions and decisions. Inner-directed children don't blame others for their unhappiness nor do they complain, or feel like victims, when things don't go smoothly. They simply do what they can to improve what they don't like and make the best of any situation.

Obviously, inner-directed children are the exception in our society, not the norm. Most children, like most adults, learn to be "outer-directed" in their thinking. Outer-directed people feel as though other people are, in some way, responsible for their happiness. They feel let down and frustrated a great deal of the time because others so rarely live up to their expectations. Outer-directed people are destined to be unhappy because they feel so powerless over their lives.

If we believe that someone or something outside ourselves has created our unhappiness, it follows that we will seek out something external to make us happy. The unfortunate result of such thinking can be a reliance on alcohol, drugs, and other "external" substances to "cure" our unhappiness. Because genuine happiness can only come from within, living an outer-directed life is inconsistent with being happy. If you want your children to be happy, self-confident, self-reliant, non-judgmental, blame-free individuals, the first step is to encourage inner-directed thinking as much as possible from this day forth.

Inner-directed thinking is an attitude toward life. It involves the recognition that each of us is unique—that each individual must decide from within, on a moment-to-moment basis, what is right. Only you can know the direction you must take and you must take responsibility for that direction.

Inner-directed people respect themselves, and others as well. They acknowledge individuality, and rarely impose their viewpoints on other people. They will kindly offer assistance when requested or needed, but will not intrude. They practice inner-directed thinking throughout their lifetime—it's as natural to them as brushing their teeth. The more habitual this becomes, the more able they are to pass this on. If your children are inner-directed, they will always show respect toward others—including yourself.

A friend of mine is one of the most inner-directed people

I know (and one of the happiest). He might visit his grand-mother less often than his brothers or sisters, but when he does, he *really* wants to be there. While his siblings are com-plaining about "having to be with grandmother," he is off enjoying himself. Recently, I had the occasion to speak with his grandmother and it was immediately obvious to me that my friend was her most treasured grandchild. When I asked her why he was so special to her, she replied with convic-tion: "Because I know that when he is here he really wants to be here. I know that he really loves me—and I love him." And while I'm sure that my friend's brothers and sisters love their grandmother, it isn't in an inner-directed way, but more out of obligation and duty.

Inner-directed thinking is an overall attitude toward life; becoming more inner-directed is as easy as changing a few habits in the way you think and behave. Below you will find a few suggestions for making the transition. The more you are able to change your own life, the more likely your chil-dren will be able to do the same.

Three Strategies to Encourage "Inner-Directedness"

1. Make seeking your approval insignificant.

All children intuitively have the need and desire to please their parents. As nice as it is that your children want to please you, approval-seeking can become a way of life. Let them know frequently that they don't need your approval to gain your love. If you want your children to be more inner-directed, begin with their relationship with you. Do they come running to you to find out whether they should feel good or bad about something? If they do, they are in the early stages of an approval-seeking lifestyle.

When children learn that they need external input to determine how they should feel or act, the tendency will not be limited to you. They will apply the same logic in their relationships with friends, teachers, other parents, and eventually in their intimate adult relationships and in their careers. Children who need lots of approval will let other people decide what they should do, how they should act, what preferences to have, and even what they are good at. I have seen many extremely talented children get frustrated with their writing, scholastic efforts, art, or athletic performance because they were basing their self-worth on what someone else thought of their performance.

The need to seek approval starts at home and it can begin to subside at home. No matter how important this is to your children, it's never too late to reverse the trend. If your children are old enough to understand, you can begin by admitting that you might have been part of the problem—that you meant no harm, but somehow you delivered the incorrect message that they need your approval before they could feel good about themselves and their efforts. I know this sounds dramatic—how many parents openly apologize to their children?—nevertheless it's a good idea. Impress upon your children that you love them, not for what they do or how well they do it, but for who they are. Let them know that you love them unconditionally, that they are special, unique, wonderful human beings. You are proud of them simply because they are alive.

You can begin to change how you interact with your children in subtle, but important, ways. If, for example, your child says to you: "Mom, Johnny said I was a stupid-head."

Instead of replying, "That wasn't very nice of him," try something like, "It doesn't matter what Johnny thinks, it only matters what you think—and I know that you know that you are terrific." Or if your child says, "Dad, if I don't make the baseball team my friends will laugh at me," respond with, "I hope that you are as proud of yourself as I am. You can feel good about yourself no matter what happens, it doesn't matter even 1% what anyone else thinks—you are a winner and I know that you know that—whether you make the team or not. I'm proud of you for making the effort. If you make the team, great, if you don't, that's okay. You'll do something else." Take the pressure off your children to live up to the expectations of others. Impress upon them how special they are to you—before they accomplish anything at all.

Back up this communication with new behavior of your own. Commit yourself to being less concerned with what others think of you. If people don't like what you're doing—that will be okay with you. You can still learn from what other people think, but you don't have to be upset by it. Not even one little bit!

I can't think of anything more important to teach my children than to do things simply because they love to. If my children try something that doesn't work out for them, and they loved doing it, then they didn't fail! To the contrary, they are winners. They have spent some precious moments of life doing something that will nurture and support them. Hopefully, they can learn from any mistakes they made, but they won't be immobilized by them.

2. *Don't compare yourself to others.*

Encourage your children not to compare themselves to others. Inner-directed people aren't concerned with how

15

they stack up. They compete only with themselves. Inner-directed people never equate their self-worth with a win-loss ratio or some competitive performance.

Children who spend valuable moments of their lives comparing themselves with others, who are always looking over their shoulder to see "how they are doing," are looking in the wrong direction. Constantly comparing yourself is a life-long prescription for frustration. There will always be someone better and there will always be someone who isn't as good—inner-directed people say "so what" to both. They know that effective living has more to do with turning inward and being proud of just who you are.

Inner-directed people *know* that they are special and unique. This is not being conceited, for they know that everyone else is special and unique, too. Why should someone who is unlike anyone who has ever lived be concerned with how he or she is doing in comparison to another?

The easiest way to help your children stop comparing themselves with others is to first stop doing it yourself. It's nothing more than a habit. When the urge comes up, remind yourself that there is no value in continuing. Then, when your children compare themselves to someone else, gently remind them that what other people do is irrelevant. Encourage them to be themselves—to love and respect who they are. If they want to get better at something, wonderful, but ask that they do so only for themselves, not to be "better than someone else."

3. *Don't take things personally.*

Few people have mastered the art of not taking things personally—but those who have are extremely happy! Taking things personally is one of the most common reasons for becoming upset and unhappy. Luckily, this common tendency stems from a relatively simple misunderstanding.

When you take a moment to reflect on your life, you will notice that any frustration, anger, disapproval, regret, disappointment, or other immobilizing feelings that you might experience have come from inside yourself, not from life itself or from other people. This is why everyday experiences will affect you differently, depending on how you feel. For example, a broken window can be either "a broken window," a simple unfortunate event, or it can be "front page news," something that ruins your entire day. The degree of upset you feel depends on what's going on inside you at the moment.

The same is true for all of us. When we are angry, we see an angry world. When we are happy, we see a happy world. When we are insecure, we tend to feel envious or jealous. What we see and how we react to life often has little to do with what we are actually seeing—and everything to do with how we are feeling. It simply makes no sense, then, to become overly upset over someone else's reaction to us. Their reaction came about as a result of how *they* were feeling—not from anything we said or did. I'm not suggesting an "avoidance attitude," not taking responsibility, but rather a new perspective on why people react the way they do.

If you can teach your children this perspective, you can help them to eliminate the frustration that usually results when someone is "upset" with them. Teach your children to learn from their mistakes and listen to what people have to say (even when they are upset), but teach them also that they don't need to take others' disapproval personally.

Again, look to change yourself as a wonderful place to

start. As you begin to take these upsets less personally, your children will learn to follow suit.

Spontaneity

Inner-directed people are spontaneous—they don't follow rigid, pre-set guidelines for living. They are committed to truth—and understand that the truth can change from moment to moment. For example, an inner-directed child may be looking forward with great anticipation to a baseball game on Saturday. But when Saturday arrives, he gets a call from his best friend asking him to go along with him and his father to the city park. If the trip to the park sounds like more fun to him, and he decides to bypass the game, he is expressing spontaneity. If you as a parent forbid your son from changing his mind (all in the name of consistency—"you made plans and you're going to stick to them"), you are telling your son not to trust his feelings, not to be spontaneous.

I'm not suggesting that a child should never stick to the plans; sometimes that's right, as is showing a commitment to others (including you), but beware of the hidden message here. I would much rather waste a few baseball game tickets than my child's self-confidence. Nothing is more important for self-esteem than how a child feels about himself and his ability to follow his own inner guidance. Spontaneity is a special part of being a child; it is a tendency inherent in all of us. If you want your child to grow up happy and self-confident, allow room for spontaneity—even if it throws you off schedule once in a while.

CHAPTER FOUR

LIVING
IN THE PRESENT

*I scarcely remember counting on happiness—I look
not for it if it not be in the present hour.*

—JOHN KEATS

C HILDREN NATURALLY "LIVE IN THE MOMENT." And because
they are such mimics, all you have to do to encourage
this is to do so yourself.

To live in the present moment means experiencing life
fully *now*. It means putting less attention on worry, concern,
regrets, mistakes, "what's wrong," things yet to be done,
things that bother you, the future, the past, and so on. Living
in the present simply means living life. Happy people know
that regardless of what happened yesterday, a month ago,
years ago—or what might happen tomorrow, next week, or
next year—*now* is where happiness will be found.

Children intuitively understand that life is a series of present moments, each meant to be experienced wholly, one
right after another. Children immerse themselves in the
present and give their full attention to the person they are
with. One of my most treasured recent memories occurred
on a Friday evening when my wife and I hired a babysitter to

watch our two-and-a-half year old daughter while we went out for the evening. My daughter and I were playing in her sandbox when the sitter arrived. When I stood to leave, she let out a fierce scream of disapproval. How dare I interrupt our fun together! She yelled and screamed and complained that she didn't want Janel—it had to be me! Shortly after my wife and I escaped, I realized that I had forgotten my car keys and I went inside to get them. I peeked out the back door, and saw that my daughter was all smiles and laughter, playing with Janel in her sandbox; once again she was absorbed in her beautiful present moments. A psychologist or cynic might say she was being manipulative towards me in an attempt to keep me with her. A happy person would recognize that she was simply voicing her strong objection. Once I left, she freely returned her focus to the here and now.

Being able to immerse yourself in the now is magical. As you do, a renewed sense of gratitude and awe begins to surface in your life. Present moment living is an antidote to worry, concern, frustration, and regret. When something really requires your concern, you will be better equipped to solve the problem, by giving it your undivided attention. And, focusing on the *now* ensures that you won't waste precious time worrying about those things that can't be changed.

Children are masters at living in the present, and it is easy to squelch this tendency. Innocently, we teach them that "someday life will be better" or that "right now isn't good enough." This kind of thinking is hard to follow, because in the moment, life is usually wonderful.

I can't tell you how many times I've caught myself rushing to the next thing with one of my children while she was perfectly happy doing exactly what she was doing. Just last week I was taking my daughter to the beach, when along the way we had minor tire trouble. We stopped at a service station to have the tire repaired and walked across the street to a park to wait. A few minutes later I was urging my daughter to come with me back to the car so that we could go to the beach to have fun. "Think of how much fun it's going to be," I said, "Come on, let's go." I have come to understand that her response was typical of someone who lives in the moment. "I don't want to go," she said. "I want to stay here." Her feeling was: Why should I get back in the car on a hot day when I am already here at a beautiful park enjoying myself outside with a bunch of other kids?

To encourage this natural tendency in your child of "living in the present," begin to appreciate yourself how wonderful living in the present really is—relearn how to live in the moment yourself. As you do, this beautiful quality in your children will flourish.

Four Strategies for Living in the Present

1. Stop what you are doing and look around.

Sounds simple—and it is—but think how infrequently you do it! How much time do you spend rushing around getting things done? As parents, we all know, there's plenty to be done. But start to make a habit of stopping at least once an hour to take a look around. It takes just a minute, but you will be amazed at the new perspective you will gain on the "rush." Slow down, have more appreciation of "moments," and you will enjoy the work you do so much more.

21

*2. The next time your child picks up some simple thing
and studies it—do it, too.*

If this sounds childish, it is! That's the whole point: to
renew your own childlike wonder and awe of the world. To
a child, everything is a potential source of interest and joy.
Anything can be picked up and studied. Whether it's a leaf,
a rock, a magazine, whatever—take a few moments to notice
something new about it.

*3. Practice being right where you are and doing exactly
what you are doing.*

Drive your car without thinking about anything else.
Don't let your mind wander to where you'd rather be, just
drive. Do the same when you are washing dishes, doing
laundry, shopping, or exercising. As you get better at "being
right where you are," you will notice an overflow into the
rest of your life. Your children will notice the change in you.
They may not be able to describe the change, but they will
notice that you are more available to them. People love to be
with people who are really with them.

4. Stop postponing gratification.

It's easy to fall into the trap of believing that you will
spend more quality time with your children after certain
conditions are met or, "later." Don't wait a minute longer.
Life isn't going to be easier or better next year; it will just be
another year. Learn to live each day as if it were your last.
Who knows? It might be. Enjoy your life while it lasts—and
you and your children will be happy together.

CHAPTER FIVE

ELIMINATING HURRY

Why should we live with such hurry and waste of life?
—HENRY DAVID THOREAU, *WALDEN*

T O HELP BRING FORTH INNER HAPPINESS in your children, try to eliminate, as much as possible, the sense of hurry and urgency in your household. It is very difficult for true happiness to exist in a hurried environment, because "hurry" is inconsistent with "being present." A child who is always being hurried doesn't have time to investigate her surroundings, to enjoy where she is right now, to reflect, or to decide whether or not she really likes something. She is rushing on to the next activity, busy looking ahead to "what's next."

Being in a hurry has more to do with state of mind than scheduling. Many parents with full-time jobs never feel hurried, and there are just as many people with no children or career who feel hurried all the time.

The hurried sense of urgency you feel will depend on how able you are to keep your attention in the present, the task at hand. If you can do what you're doing without also thinking about "what's next," or "how much more you have to do," you will be on your way to a more peaceful life—and so will your children.

The solution to all "hurry" is to become more "present-moment-oriented." You won't feel hurried, no matter how busy you are, as soon as you forget about all you have to do, and instead stay immersed in the present moments of your life.

Hurry is a bad habit—letting your mind wander away from where you are to where you are going next—and next—and next. As long as you continue thinking about things that are yet to be done you will feel hurried. But when you can recognize the dynamic, and begin to pull the reins in on your own thinking, remaining more and more in the moment, that sense of hurry you normally feel will diminish until eventually it fades away.

Children are rarely in a hurry. It's always us, the parents, who want to leave and go on to the next thing. Recently, I watched a father in a toy store urge his daughter, "hurry up," "come on," "it's time to go," and so forth. The feeling coming from this father was urgent—as though there were some emergency. Ten minutes later I saw the same man at the bookstore doing the very same thing! He wasn't *really* in a hurry. There was no emergency. But he felt hurried, and so did his daughter.

We all do the same thing to our children often, to different degrees. The effect of this "hurry" on our own life is bad enough, but the effect on our children can be devastating. This false sense of urgency teaches our children that *life is an emergency!* Life *isn't* an emergency, but the sense of hurry that we parents feel will promote a wrong sense of hurry in our children.

Obviously, there are times when you do need to do something quickly—but try to save it for those rare occasions when it's truly necessary. The truth is, most hurry can be eliminated. Intentionally slow yourself down, bring yourself back to right here, where you are now, and stay there. Try it today. It's easier than you think. When you train your mind to be right here and enjoy this moment, you won't have room in your mind for all the hurried thoughts that you are used to producing.

I used to be in a hurry most of the time. Today, though I am far busier than I used to be, I feel less rushed. I have a busier schedule, but I'm seldom in a hurry.

> *Until we teach them differently, children*
> *know that life isn't an emergency.*

Once, we all felt that life was an enjoyable, creative experience—we didn't wait for some later date when all our work would be done and everything complete—we enjoyed ourselves. As children, the simplest things are fun. Shopping, walking in the park, collecting leaves, reading a book, practicing a skill, or looking at birds and insects are all wonderful expressions of a calm sense of creativity—until we become convinced that these activities are merely stepping stones to something better.

The elimination of hurry is critical to happiness because we all need time to absorb our world and our surroundings. Children need time to investigate, imagine, explore, notice, perceive, understand. But they can't if they are constantly forced to hurry; rush on to the next thing, the next, and the next, like a hamster on a wheel. Rushing around takes away from a child's inherent, unhurried feeling of happiness, curiosity, and creativity.

25

You Can Slow Down

That sense of hurry you may have developed is reversible. It's never too late. You will be amazed at how readily your children will respond—no matter what their age—to a less panicked lifestyle. Just as hurry promotes hurry, so does calmness promote calmness. A few weeks of genuine calm can reverse a lifetime of hurried panic.

Creativity is an inherent quality in everyone, just waiting to be expressed. All your children need for you is a good example, and your permission to let it show.

"But I'm Really Busy"

I know you're busy—all parents are busy. This is all the more reason to take to heart what I am saying. Believe it or not, you will get done twice the work in half the time as soon as you get beyond the distracting sense of hurry as you go about your life.

As your mind begins to slow down, new options will develop in your life that you were "too busy" to see before—including new freedom in your schedule. *Calm, unhurried people are far more productive and creative than hurried people.* The reason: Unhurried people see the big picture better; they see the possibilities, they remain calm in a crisis. Unhurried people can access their own wisdom and common sense easier than rushed people, because they aren't as caught up in their own leaping thinking.

Don't you agree that your children would rather spend one relaxed hour with you than a whole day running around with a pervasive sense of hurry? Being with a hurried person, even one you love, is stressful. But to be with a calm person is delightful and reassuring.

And you will also benefit from a new commitment to a non-rushed life. As you immerse yourself in the present moment with your children, you will enjoy them like never before. Practice a less hurried life, especially around your children, starting today. You will begin to enjoy life as a parent more than you have been—and your children will appreciate that.

Stop to Smell the Roses

"Life is what happens to you while you're busy making other plans." But we keep thinking that once we get everything done, we'll enjoy life then. But let's face it, even when your life is over you'll still probably have work in your "In Basket," things you still have to do—you'll never get it all done. So it's okay to start enjoying your life today. *Life isn't an emergency.* You can still work hard, have goals and dreams, get a lot done, and meanwhile you will enjoy the process. Life is not a dress rehearsal for some other day. The play has begun: appreciate your life—it is the only time you'll ever have.

If you want your children to be calm and creative individuals, teach them to take time every day to stop and smell the roses. Literally! Stop whatever you are doing and take a look at your garden. Notice the beauty. Appreciate this life, this natural beauty, all the people you know. And share your new sense of calm and appreciation with your children.

Demonstrate that you are calm and creative and you enjoy your life right now. You are the best example your children have. Show them, by example, to be right where they are, to enjoy life in a non-rushed manner. It's really okay to slow down a little, appreciate the little things in life. Be calm and happy, even when things are less than perfect.

The Greatest Gift

Give your children a less hurried life. This doesn't necessarily mean fewer activities, although it might. It means being more present, less scattered. As you practice the unhurried life in your home, an immediate shift will occur in your child's sense of calm, which will open the door to creativity.

Seven Ways to Eliminate Hurry in Your House

1. Be patient.

Impatience encourages "hurry" in your children. Take a look at the subtle ways that you are impatient. Make a commitment to change. Are you angry when something doesn't arrive in the mail? Do you tailgate slower drivers? Do you say things like "hurry up" more than you really need to? Do you complain about people who move slowly? Do you rush through meals? Do you start clearing the dishes before everyone is finished eating? These and hundreds of examples like them are the little ways in which you show your children to hurry through life. Notice your own patterns. Make an honest commitment to practice patience.

2. Expose your children to quiet and relaxing activities.

Give your children the opportunity to explore inner-oriented activities—meditation, yoga, reading, visualization. These are some of the most powerful techniques known to any of us, and are both calming and extremely creative. These, and similar activities encourage children to investigate their own inner worlds and bring forth their inherent happiness. Most children of any age absolutely love these "non-activities."

3. Schedule nonstructured time in the day.

Most families are so structured with activities that there is little time to simply "be." It's important for children to have time, every single day, where there is nothing going on at all. This gives them the time to practice being creative, to use their imaginations, to see what it's like to do nothing, and to come up with new ideas.

4. Encourage alone time.

Happiness is individual. Happy people are not like other people—they are like themselves. Children need time to be alone so they can get to know themselves. If your child is playing happily alone, leave her alone! Don't interfere unless you absolutely have to. Be prepared to change plans at the last minute on those occasions when your child is playing by herself. It is far more important for her to continue exploring the world she is creating than to stick to some rigid plan.

5. Show your children that you don't need television.

Some television is fine, but avoid depending on it to keep you company. Be flexible; miss your own favorite programs once in a while. Have plenty of nights without the TV on at all.

6. Celebrate silence.

Schedule in quiet time throughout the day—moments when you simply sit and think. Do this frequently each day with your children. Take time to notice the beauty of silence.

7. Praise investigation.

If your child is looking at something, try to stop what you are doing and investigate it, too. Tell him how wonderful you think exploring is, and ask him to tell you about it.

I remember the time my daughter and I met my wife one day for lunch. Afterwards, I had intended to bring my daughter to the park, but she became totally involved with some rocks behind the parking lot. Rather than rush off to the park simply because we had planned to do so, we sat right there, together, and played with those rocks for well over an hour. We never did make it to the park but, boy, did we have fun.

CHAPTER SIX

QUIET TIME

Study to be quiet, and to do your own business.

—ST. PAUL

ETTING ASIDE A FEW MINUTES a day for quiet time with your child can be one of the most beautiful and rewarding activities you engage in as a parent. Quiet time can just be a few quality minutes when your life slows down and you absorb yourself in the present moment, when your entire focus of attention is on the wonder of your child and the awe of life. Quiet time is a short period of time, somewhere between three and ten minutes, where you simply sit quietly together with your child and do nothing but appreciate the beauty of the moment. There is very little structure to quiet time, it is simply a time for both of you to settle down and take a few moments to appreciate life and each other.

Quiet time is appropriate at any age; infants love it, and your teenagers often need it. Drop what you are doing, stop whatever you are thinking about, and take a break from your routine. There is nothing more earth-shattering or mysterious about it, no right or wrong way to do it, but it is so important to your health and happiness.

As you make a habit of "quiet time," you will develop your own way of doing it. When I sit with my toddler, for our quiet time together, we settle down on the couch or the floor. We don't roughhouse or play—we just sit there quietly, alone together. If my daughter is in a hyperactive mood, we might start by reading a book or listening to music until she (and, often, I) settle down a little. As I begin to feel more calm and appreciative, I bring my attention inward, and take my mind off my concerns, worries, expectations, goals, all the things I have to do. I try to let all distractions leave my mind and focus instead on my breathing and the feeling of love I have toward my beautiful child. As I do this, I watch my daughter and usually notice that she, too, is becoming calmer and more relaxed. Obviously, I don't know what she is thinking about, but I do know that she is feeling peaceful and happy. I can see it in her eyes and in her smile.

Carve Out Your Own Quiet Time

It doesn't matter how you go about relaxing and quieting down. The important thing is to try it. If you are like most of us, you will be amazed at how easy it is to slow down, take a break, and enjoy the quiet of the moment. These few minutes a day can serve to remind you and your child that it's okay to stop "doing" for a few minutes—and what often happens when you stop "doing" is you feel free to simply "be." Give yourself permission to step back and notice the beauty of life.

Quiet time is often most effective when it isn't planned. The best time for a quiet period is when you are the most frantic, hurried, worried, or rushed. That's when you really need a booster shot of perspective. A few minutes will usually put you back on track to where you really want to be with your child. Quiet time will provide you with the wisdom and perspective you need to move through the rest of your day much more gracefully and with more appreciation. It is the perfect antidote for anger, frustration, pessimism, concern, or worry.

If you did nothing differently in your life other than taking these few special minutes a day together, you would notice substantial changes in your child's calmness and appreciation for life. This special time will feel so soothing and comforting that each of you—both separately and together—will begin to seek this quiet feeling more often in your lives.

As you begin to incorporate quiet time into your daily life, you may be pleasantly surprised at how this new appreciation of calmness will appear, little changes such as a renewed appreciation of nature or silence may become obvious. A little quiet time each day goes a long way. You can build up a "bank account" of calmness to carry you through your day.

One positive byproduct of this special time is that both you and your children will begin to notice little things about one another that were always there, that you might not have paid attention to before. Things like the subtle shades of color in your children's eyes, the texture of their skin, the shape of their ears, even the unique way they breathe. If you speak to each other during this time, you may notice certain vocal mannerisms and qualities for the very first time. You will get an enormous amount of new information from one another, which can generate enhanced appreciation of one another.

Why didn't we notice these qualities about each other before? It's not because we don't care or love each other, but there is so much competition from our environment. A quiet time allows for the luxury of slowing everything down. It gives us the time and space to notice the unique and wonderful child who has been right there beside us all along.

This quiet period is astoundingly effective in bringing forth calmness, creativity, and happiness in children—magic. I find that a genuinely quiet time of five minutes or so—in which I'm just sitting calmly with my child—generates as much calm in me as a week-long vacation in Hawaii! The purpose of a vacation is to take your mind off your responsibilities and give you time for yourself. Unfortunately, it takes many people the first three or four days of their vacation to slow down. You can learn to take a "daily vacation" simply by getting yourself into a more relaxed state of mind. The more you practice, eventually, you will be able to find that quiet place inside yourself at will. And your children can learn to do the very same thing.

Quiet time has become the most treasured few minutes of my day. I look forward to it—and more importantly, the effects of this special time have become integrated into the rest of my life and the life of my child. I have also noticed an enormous positive change in my daughter. She has responded to our special time together in ways that I never dreamed possible. For example, she will now sit quietly with me for several minutes and then reach over and give me a big hug. I feel her appreciation and love for me growing deeper. We are sharing something that every parent dreams of: silent respect, mutual admiration, and love.

If you think about it, it's obvious why a daily dose of quietness would bring parents and children closer. We all know that children love our attention, especially when it's undivided.

But how many of us, in the midst of our busy lives, can really offer our children this special gift? Likewise, how many of us ever allow ourselves to be the object of someone's focused attention? Quiet time is no more than giving and receiving genuine undivided attention.

This special time for you and your children will set the mood for happiness to thrive. It will open new doors of creativity, gratitude, and love—for both of you.

Acting as Mirrors for Our Children

During your quiet time, your child's level of calmness will tend to match yours. This matching or mimicking of energy is commonly referred to as mirroring.

The concept of mirroring suggests that in any given interaction between two people, there are only two possible dynamics. The first possibility is that the calmer individual will become increasingly hyper to mirror the more anxious person. The second possibility is just the opposite: the more hyper of the two will calm down.

By giving ourselves intentional time to calm down, we gain control over this mirroring process. If we are paying attention to our own energy, and the energy of our child, we can easily sense who is the calmer of the two. (Make no mistake: There will be times when the calmer one is your child!) Once we have a sense of the relative calmness in the room, we can balance all that energy into a more relaxed state.

"Quality Time"

Who wouldn't love to have more quality time with their children? But just what is quality time? Isn't it time to simply enjoy our children? Many of us have confused quality time with *doing* something. But you don't need to be doing anything at all to be grateful and happy that you are a parent.

Quiet time *is* quality time. It's time to reflect, to notice, to appreciate, and to love. It's easy to fall into the trap of thinking that "someday" you will take the time to enjoy—someday when all the details of your life are worked out—someday when the pressure is off—someday when things are different. But there's always going to be a "someday." Problems straightened out will always be replaced by others that need your attention. Begin appreciating your life now. The daily practice of quiet time is a great place to start.

CHAPTER SEVEN

CHILDREN
AND MOODS

*Time cools, time clarifies; no mood can be maintained
quite unaltered through the course of hours.*

—THOMAS MANN

THE SUN COMES UP IN THE MORNING—the sun goes down in the evening. The ocean tide comes in—the ocean tide goes out. And children (and adults) all have moods. Moods are a fact of life.

Everyone who lives experiences mood swings—everyone. In higher moods, or "feeling states," people have the greatest perspective, possessed of wisdom, kindness, and compassion. It is in our higher moods that we make the best decisions about our lives, our goals, and our problems. And it is in our higher moods when we do our best job as parents. When we feel great, parenting is effortless, rewarding, and a lot of fun.

In lower moods, life seems difficult; we see more problems and fewer solutions. We have little perspective, common sense, or wisdom. When we are stuck in a low mood we often make bad decisions and lots of mistakes, and we have little appreciation for life.

When we are in a high mood, parenting is a delight; it's fun and rewarding, worth the challenge and effort. In higher moods we rise to the occasion; we have plenty of gratitude for our children and for the gift of parenthood. In our lower moods, however, parenting can seem extremely difficult, not worth it, demanding, boring, restricting, and so forth.

And while it has always been, and always will be, true that life appears vastly different depending on how we feel, few of us know enough to respect the power of moods as a way to understand what is occurring. We make the mistake of believing that life has suddenly changed for the worse! When you feel good, life is relatively easy. Everything goes more smoothly, including your chores and responsibilities as a parent. When you feel great, and your child breaks something, it's easy for you to be patient and understanding. When you feel terrific and your children make a mess, it's far easier for you to ask them in a nice and loving way to either help clean it up—or to go outside and play.

When your mood is low, *anything* can bother you. When your mood is high, you can handle almost anything that comes up with some degree of compassion and understanding.

What I am sharing with you here isn't new—but it is important to understand. The point is this: When you are in a low mood, you are going to have virtually no patience. Life is going to seem urgent and demanding, difficult and bothersome, nothing more than a series of problems to overcome—and your child is one of your primary problems! Your decision-making capacity is going to be limited and your thinking is going to be clouded. Sound bad? It is—but this is what all of us are up against in our lowest moods.

To compound the problem, it is in our lowest moods,

when we are least equipped to do so, that we will feel most compelled to attempt to solve our problems. Really! Strange as it seems, most people have their most serious and important discussions while they are in a low mood! The implication of this fact is quite scary. Big decisions regarding your children are often made without your psychological bearings, when you have very little perspective. Again, the reason for this is simple: When you feel bad, life seems urgent. And, as compelling as low moods can be, you can begin to recognize when you are in one and what will come about as a result.

Five Ways to Handle Low Moods

While we can't make our low moods disappear, we can learn to protect ourselves against them. Since we know exactly how we are going to see life when we are in a low mood—pessimistic—we can make allowances. The following is a list of guidelines to follow whenever you feel down.

1. Distrust what you think and feel in a low mood.

"Low mood thinking" isn't worth paying attention to. You are always going to see the problems of life instead of the beauty when you are down. Strive to understand the predicament you are in, while you are in it, and wait until you feel better before you react. Usually, even a few minutes will help. You will begin to feel better if you don't think too much about how bad you feel.

2. Don't make important decisions when you feel bad.

When you are down, you have extremely limited access to your wisdom and common sense, and your decisions will reflect this lower state of mind. Again, wait a little while until you feel better before making any commitments. If you absolutely must make a decision while you are down, do so with the understanding that you aren't seeing life clearly.

3. Don't take things personally.

This is far easier said than done. In low moods it will seem to you that life is all about you. You will have a strong tendency to take everything personally—especially your children's behavior. Keep in mind that when you feel better, you will see the identical situation quite differently.

4. Keep in mind that life will look better soon.

Notice I said "look" better instead of "get" better. Life itself usually doesn't change all that much from day to day. What does change is your mood. When you feel low, you will be unable to see the beauty in life and you will have a limited perspective. Remember that every time you have felt down before, the fog has lifted and you somehow felt better. Keep faith that, in time, you will again.

5. Admit that you're "out to lunch" when you are in a low mood.

Don't justify your "right to feel bad." Recognize that you feel that way, and move through it. The greatest protection you can have against low moods is to understand, before the fact, what is going to happen to you when you feel bad. Once you're "in it," it's too late!

In order to live gracefully through a low mood, admit that you aren't seeing things clearly, and wait it out until you feel better.

40

Respect Your Children and Their Moods

So far, I've focused on how low moods distort our thinking as parents. But keep in mind that your children have mood swings too! In some ways, children have more perspective about their moods than do adults. What I mean by this is that children don't usually "hold on" to their low moods. When they feel bad, you usually hear about it in one way or another. But a minute or two later (or an hour or two later), they will pull themselves out of it as if it never happened. Compare this to an adult who keeps himself in a low mood by dwelling on how bad he feels, and talking about it to his friends and family! Children are as guilty as adults of believing the reality of what they feel in a low mood, but they are more able to forget about it.

Low Moods Are Experienced Uniquely

While the characteristics of a low mood are similar for everyone, each of us will experience and play out our low mood in our own way. When I'm in a low mood, my tendency is to rush around, believing that there isn't enough time. When my wife is in a low mood, she will become quiet and withdrawn. We feel equally bad, but we experience it differently. When our toddler is in a low mood she gets testy and demanding, whereas one of her best friends, another toddler, becomes very sad and withdrawn when she's in a low mood.

If you want to teach your children to be happy, tell them it's okay to have low moods. Your children are every bit as confused and insecure in their low moods (maybe even

41

more so) than you are in yours—and they don't usually know what's happening either. When children feel bad, when they are in a low mood, they do the only thing they know how to do: react to how they are feeling. They "act out" their frustration through their behavior. If their low mood is making them feel angry, they act angry. If they are feeling insecure, they act out by sulking or pouting.

When you begin to understand the incredible power that moods have over your children, it begins to make sense to you why your children are acting in ways that you don't like. In short, they can't help it—they can't help it anymore than you or I can help it when we are down. Once you understand the delusionary capacity of low moods, it won't frustrate you so much when your children act out their low moods. In fact, you will learn to *expect* it.

When your children are in a low mood, they will simply react to how they feel. The bad feeling they are experiencing comes from within themselves and has little to do with you. In a very real sense, you can blame your child's behavior on her mood. Don't take it personally. It's not your fault, and you don't have to worry about it. Like you, they will pull out of this low mood as they have thousands of times before, if you simply let them be.

Does this mean you should always excuse your child's behavior simply because they are feeling low? Of course not. You still have to teach them how you would like them to act. Understanding their moods, however, gives you better perspective when deciding how to respond to their actions. It allows you to make allowances for their behavior because you know what is going on from a psychological perspective.

There is very little you can do to help your child out of a low mood. Because moods are a fact of life, the best any of us can do is understand what is happening. Often, the most appropriate course of action to take is to leave her alone. Don't ignore her completely, but do give her a little distance. Once her attention is off how bad she feels, she will be on the road to recovery. It all happens quite naturally and usually quickly. What keeps a person, any person, in a low mood is too much attention on how she is feeling.

Two Scenarios

Let me give you two everyday examples to illustrate how this works. Let's assume in both examples that a five-year-old girl, Kimmy, is in a foul mood. Here are two possible conversations:

Kimmy: Mom I'm bored. What can I do?

Mom: What's wrong, Honey?

Kimmy: Nothing's wrong, what can I do?

Mom: Oh come on Honey, I know you. Something's wrong.

Kimmy: I'm bored, Mom. I want to go outside.

Mom: You can't go outside now, it's too cold.

Kimmy: Why isn't there anything to do around here?

Mom: There are plenty of things to do. Why don't you play with your dolls?

Kimmy: I don't want to play with my dolls.

Mom: Why don't you play with your new blocks?

Kimmy: I don't like my blocks.

Mom: Honey, what's wrong? Do you want to talk about it?

Kimmy: Nothing's wrong.

In this rather typical dialogue, the conversation was obviously going nowhere. Kimmy is in a bad mood. Nothing her mother says is going to help her, and in fact, if you look at the conversation closely, you will see that the mother's well-meaning attempts were only making matters worse. Her emphasis on the idea that something was "wrong" was fueling the fire. The mother's suggestions were being heard by Kimmy to mean that she does indeed need help in finding something to do; they were reinforcing the idea that something was wrong. When a child is in a "bad mood," it's often difficult to remember that when she is in a "good mood," she always finds something to do—she is never bored. Likewise, when she is in a "good mood," she rarely complains. Your child's mood will dictate her behavior! As long as you remember this fact, you are, in effect, protected. You won't panic when your child is low, and you won't take her mood so personally. You'll know that it's nothing more than a bad mood.

Now let's consider an alternative dialogue.

Kimmy: Mom I'm bored. What can I do?

Mom: I'm sure you'll find something to do. You always do. You're so creative.

Kimmy: I am not. I'm bored. What can I do?

Mom: I have faith in you, Kimmy, and I love you. You go ahead and find something to do—I'll be in the kitchen.

Can you see the difference? Here, the mother has been equally loving, but she has put the problem into Kimmy's hands—she feels no urgency to solve it. She understands that Kimmy is in a low mood. So what! This happens from

44

time to time—and every time it happens Kimmy pulls herself out of it; she has faith that this time is no exception. She still loves and cares for Kimmy and she knows that Kimmy's low moods never last too long. Just like anyone else, whenever Kimmy feels low, she will feel somewhat victimized, as though she has no creativity. She will believe she needs someone else to solve her problems which, in fact, can be solved by herself.

Did you also notice that in the second conversation, the mother was letting her daughter know that she has faith in her? She flat-out told Kimmy, "You can do it." She also let Kimmy know that her problem wasn't as serious as she thought. In the first conversation, the mother went along with the idea that something was wrong. The more the mother bought into the dynamic, the more convinced Kimmy was.

Children need to know that we, their parents, have faith in them. When we understand the tricky, deceptive nature of low moods, we can teach our children that their "problems" are not as formidable and serious as they thought.

You can have enormous compassion and understanding for your children when they are down, but you don't need to feel sorry for them. Moods are a fact of life, and they shouldn't be feared. All happy people have moods, including very low moods. The lesson you want to teach your children is to not take those low moods too seriously. And the best way you can teach this is to demonstrate to them that you are okay with their moods. Show them that you don't panic at the first sign of trouble. It's no longer going to be "front page news" when your child is down!

Likewise, don't be so concerned yourself when you are down. When you feel down, admit it. Let your kids know that you are human, and you too have low moods. But you know that they always go away. And when they do, life looks much better.

A Lesson from a Parenting Class

A friend and colleague of mine was asked to teach the tenth hour of a ten-hour parenting class for new parents. The first question he asked the class was, "How many of you feel as though you have received valuable information from this class?" All fifty parents raised their hands. Next, he asked, "How many of you, when you have been in a great mood and feeling really positive about life, did all the things that have been suggested to you here, naturally—even before you learned this information?" Again, all fifty parents raised their hands. Finally, he asked, "How many of you, when you drop into a really low mood, feeling insecure and negative, think you will be able to implement the information you have learned here?" Not a single parent raised a hand! "Then it seems to me," said my friend, "that effective parenting has little to do with techniques and information, and has everything to do with feeling positive and knowing when you don't feel positive."

I couldn't agree more with his conclusion! When you are down in the dumps, the best you can do is recognize that you are in a low mood, and do the best you can, given that fact. Soon, *if you don't think about it too much,* you will feel better. And when you do, parenting will seem more effortless and enjoyable. No one can avoid low moods altogether, but parents with wisdom have the humility to admit when they are in one.

Teach your children to respect the power of moods. They will be "grateful" when they feel good and "graceful" when they feel bad, and you will have taught them a valuable lesson. If your children can learn not to take low moods (including yours) too seriously, they will be on their way to a happier life.

CHAPTER EIGHT

JUDGMENT-FREE ACTIVITY

All work and no play makes Jack a dull boy.

—James Howell

I N ORDER TO FOSTER HAPPINESS in your children, let each day have at least one activity that is completely judgment-free. Many parents, upon hearing this suggestion, reply, "I don't judge my children." Before you also make this conclusion, let me define what I mean by judgment-free.

To me, judgment-free implies a carefree attitude, not measuring progress or wondering if what your child is doing is leading him anywhere. It means not questioning whether his activity is in line with goals and aspirations, or whether he is performing an activity correctly. It means not worrying about what other people think.

A judgment-free activity can be anything—swinging, climbing a tree, petting an animal. It is time in which you and your child do something together that is not goal-oriented. I know this sounds strange in our goal-oriented culture, but this kind of time can be so important to the development of your child's creativity and happiness.

Happiness stems from a clear, fresh mind that sees everything new—a mind that is not distracted by negative thoughts or preconceived ideas, that doesn't define itself by past actions. Perhaps the best way to demonstrate this unusual idea is to study the opposite extreme—a busy or obsessive mind.

You probably already know what a busy mind feels like: overwhelmed, heavy, and concerned. *A busy mind has no room for creativity and fresh thought.* It's too busy, hurried, evaluating everyone's performance, especially its own. It tends to go over the same set of facts and problems over and over until it reaches some sort of decision, which is often similar to a decision it made before. It then goes on to the next set of facts and does the very same thing. A person with an overly busy mind is incapable of enjoying life because a busy mind cannot stay in the moment—it is either wondering how it is doing or it's on to the next thing.

For your child to live a creative, happy life, she will need to foster her ability to remain in the present moment, to see new ideas, new solutions, new answers, and new possibilities. But she will not be able to do this if her mind is busy reviewing her past or imagining her future.

Fortunately, this ability to see life fresh, to see "the new" is something all children are born with. It will come forth automatically when the mind can quiet down and be brought back to the present moment. As this happens, the inherent, inborn happiness will begin to bubble up and any negative self-judgment will fade away. Your job as a parent is to give permission and guidance to remain as much as possible in the present moment.

The happiest, most creative individuals are usually very young children. Their creative play is almost unbelievable.

To them, everything is fun, everything is a miracle, a potential source of enjoyment. Why? Why can young children have so much fun and remain lighthearted while adults rarely allow themselves the same luxury? The answer is simple: Youngsters aren't thinking about the implications of their activity; they're not wondering how it applies to the future or whether or not it's getting them anywhere. Adults do the opposite. They rarely try something new without evaluating their performance.

A few weeks ago I was jogging by a tennis court where two men were finishing up a game. One said to the other, "I'm giving up this game; I'm just not getting any better." The other replied, "But I thought you loved tennis." The response: "I do, but so what? Loving the game isn't getting me anywhere." Sadly, this is the attitude of many adults. If something isn't leading us somewhere, (wherever that might be), then it must not be worth doing. Most of us forget that it's okay to do something for no other reason than the fact that we enjoy it.

As children grow up, this attitude is imposed upon them until, at some point, they forget how to simply "be." They forget how to enjoy life in the here and now, and how to do things just for the fun of it.

The idea of at least one judgment-free activity per day is one step toward reversing this dynamic. It demonstrates to your children that it's all right to simply "be" for at least a few minutes a day—to transform from a "human doing" back to a "human being." Don't worry that your children will become lazy or apathetic. They won't. In fact, the opposite will happen. *Children who are given permission to "be" feel free to become all they can be.* They feel less critical of themselves, so their minds are freed to be more creative, to "fail," to express new thoughts and ideas, to explore possibilities.

You may need to help your child let go of his own judgment of himself. Gently encourage and guide him to stop thinking about his performance so much—not only during this judgment-free period, but all through the day. Show him that you are doing the same thing in your life. Remember, you are your child's first teacher, and your example is primary. Show him that you have periods of time when you're not thinking about how you're doing, when nothing is on your mind, when you don't care whether or not you're good at something. While sometimes it's appropriate to strive for a goal and to work hard, it's also desirable at times to reflect on nothing at all, to allow your mind to rest so that new ideas can come into your head.

The judgment-free period should have no structure. Do it when you wake up in the morning, before bedtime, or anytime in between. Try to make it a priority in your day.

Seven Guidelines to Becoming More Judgment-Free

1. Do things "just for fun." Encourage your children to do the same.

Don't be obsessed with achievement. Childhood is too short to be consumed with goals. Ride a bike, not to see how far you can go, but because it's fun to ride a bike. Draw a picture, not to win an art contest, but to enjoy the colors. Take a walk in the woods or the park, not to test your expertise at labeling birds, but because it feels good to experience nature.

2. Point out to your children (and praise) people who look like they are having fun for fun's sake.

Seek out people who appear to enjoy life; there are plenty of them and we can all learn from them. If you want to learn about happiness, study happy people. If you see someone having fun in a park, take a look. Show your child that you respect and admire people who enjoy their life.

3. Try new activities.

Life is not a mechanical process, filled up with the same activities day after day. Indicate that you truly enjoy new things, new people, new places.

4. Avoid asking: "Why are you doing that?" unless you are genuinely and completely interested.

Questions like that only reinforce the idea that there must always be a purposeful reason for doing something. When your child asks you, "Why are you doing that?" respond by saying, "Because I enjoy it." Not, "Because I have to" or, "Because someone has to do it."

5. Demonstrate gratitude for the simple things in life.

Show your child that you are a person who is truly grateful for the simple, good things in life: a sunset, rain, insects, birds, children laughing, or a kind gesture. Be grateful to have a child and let him know that you are grateful. Appreciative people are happy; they see the beauty in life while others miss it. They have trained themselves to look for what is right with what they see, and what is beautiful. An ungrateful person is too busy comparing it to something else better.

6. *Learn from others.*

Be openminded, open to suggestion. Don't get stuck on seeing and doing things in a certain way. Happy people learn from others; they know there is always more than one way to do something and to look at something. Happy people use other people's ideas as a springboard to ideas of their own. They love education and learning because it inspires new growth and potential.

7. *Be flexible.*

Be willing to change your mind. Stay committed to "truth," not to being consistent just for the sake of it. Show your children that you can be both liberal and conservative, that you are willing to admit when you are wrong. You are showing your children, by example, what life is all about. Be a shining example of a truly happy person.

CHAPTER NINE

LOOKING
FOR THE GOOD

If there is anything that we wish to change in the child,
we should first examine it and see whether it is not
something that could be better changed in ourselves.

—CARL JUNG

B E ON THE LOOKOUT FOR THE GOOD in your children. Seek out the best that your children have to offer. Look for what is right—the ways in which your children are expressing their unique creativity. When you do notice the good in your children, let them know about it! Use praise frequently—many times an hour if possible, and do this from the very first day of their life. Children learn at an early age how much you, the parent, respect their uniqueness. It is impossible to give a child too much praise, and its connection to happiness is strong. Children who receive a great deal of praise will see themselves as praiseworthy. Children who have been told repeatedly how special they are will see themselves as special and will trust their own abilities and sense of direction.

Looking for "what's right" with your child and with what she is doing, encourages creative exploration. In a very real sense, it gives her permission to pursue her own endeavors and dreams. When your child says "Look, Mommy," stop what you are doing and look. Tell her how wonderful she is. Find something about what she is doing that is terrific.

All children have an intuitive, inherent sense of happiness and creativity. What they need from you is permission to go right on believing they are wonderful. Provide them with plenty of reinforcement emphasizing how terrific they are, especially when they do things their own way. Remind them that they are not like everyone else; they need be true only to themselves. All children will need to learn also to follow rules, but don't take it too far. Personal safety and respect for others are extremely important, but following someone else's path or way of doing something is not!

Panning for Gold

There will be times when it seems impossible to find the good in what your children are doing—when it seems far more appropriate to criticize. When your children are complaining, whining, or acting disrespectful, it can be frustrating, if not downright aggravating. The truth is that these are the times when it is *most* critical that you be looking for the good. Instead of reminding your child that he is often bored, ask him what he would prefer to be doing. If your child is habitually late or forgetful, *don't* reinforce the problem by saying: "You are hopeless" or "You are always late." To do so is the worst thing to do. Instead, take responsibility to elicit greater creativity. You know your child has a creative answer within himself; remind him of this and help him find it.

Parenting can be like "panning for gold." If you have ever seen someone panning for gold, or if you have ever tried it

56

yourself, you know that well over 99% of what you see *isn't* gold. But to strike it rich, you have to disregard the 99% and focus your attention on the 1%. The better you get at the process, the greater the reward. So too with your children. The more able you are to focus on what's right instead of what's wrong, the more you will see how genuinely wonderful your children are. More importantly, your children will see what's right with themselves; they will break through their own barriers and limitations.

Occasionally, looking for the good will require you to expand your own boundaries and transcend your usual way of seeing things. Let's suppose, for example, that you yourself have a problem with being alone; you feel that being alone is "bad," that it's better to be with someone else. If you feel this way, you may well assume that company is what your child prefers. You may be wrong! Your child may *love* to be alone. She may enjoy the "space." When your child wants to be alone, you may feel there is something wrong with her. You might badger her with questions like, "What's wrong?" or "Is everything all right?" While these questions may be caring, be careful, because they can also squelch happiness and creativity.

Don't let your own beliefs interfere with your child's uniqueness. Remember the hidden messages in what you convey to your child. Acting concerned, when your child simply wants to be alone, can actually teach her to think that there is something wrong with wanting to be alone, that there is something wrong with the way she feels. It can foster dependence on other people, and teach her to be like you rather than act like herself.

Happy people often wish to be alone, to play, to sit and

think and talk to themselves. Children need alone time to come up with new ideas. Keep in mind that if something *is* bothering your child, it is often more appropriate to let her resolve her own inner conflict. By allowing her to do so, you are giving her the message that she is in control of her own life, and is capable of solving her own problems. Be available to your child should she want you, but let her make that determination herself.

Even infants, who need almost constant physical and emotional love and support, can enjoy a few moments alone in their crib or cradle. Even a minute or two represents a long time in a baby's life. My wife and I found that our first-born daughter *loved* to be left alone in her crib when she woke up in the morning and after her afternoon nap. We would listen to her through the baby monitor, giggling and playing with her stuffed animals. Before we recognized this preference, one of us would almost always rush in to get her. It took a while to learn that she wanted nothing to do with us when she first woke up; she wanted to be alone. After her brief "alone period," she welcomed us with open arms and laughter. Every child is different, of course, and some want you to rush right in to make them feel secure—but there will be times, if you look for them, when your child will prefer to be alone.

Dealing with Frustration

When your child becomes frustrated, don't be too quick to jump to the rescue and assume that he needs you. He may not! I know it can be tempting to do everything for your child, especially when he is frustrated, but doing so is giving him the hidden message, "I can't do it without you." For children to be happy, they need to know that they are capable of anything and everything. Being happy requires an inner-directed attitude toward life—the feeling that "I don't always need others to do things for me." Even if your help is motivated by a feeling of love, which it most certainly is, it may very well be teaching your child to be self-defeating. Let your child know how capable he is to do things for himself. Teach him to trust and value himself.

The Hidden Messages in What We Say

Be aware of your choice of words. It is possible that you are giving your child negative messages even when your intention is 100% pure and loving.

Consider the father who is sitting anxiously in the bleachers, watching his youngster play Little League baseball. Because he wants to encourage his child to do well, he yells out a phrase of encouragement: "Don't miss!" What he is doing—albeit innocently—is encouraging his child to miss the ball! As the father's voice is heard across the field, a scenario forms. The bat swings and hits nothing but air—in short, misses! But if the father changed his wording so that it worked as he intended, he might say, "All right, kid—hit that ball a mile!" This subtle change of wording will encourage the young ball player to form an inner picture of that bat smacking the ball over the fence—which will make it more likely to occur.

Let's look at another, similar example. Suppose a mother wants to prevent her young child from spilling a glass of milk onto the new living room carpet. She warns the child, "Whatever you do, DON'T SPILL THAT MILK! You know the rest; the child spills the milk exactly in the place the parent mentioned. Why? Luck? Sabotage? Lack of love? No, and neither is it bad parenting. It's simply a misunderstanding in the formation of mental imaging. Upon hearing the negative instructions, a short but powerful inner exercise took place. In a sense, the child practices spilling the milk.

Changing your choice of words to: "I'm so happy that you're always careful when you carry your milk across the room" will help form a positive image in the child's mind, and encourage a positive response.

Affirmations

An affirmation is a positive assertion—a word or series of words, either written or spoken, that we can repeat to ourselves. Affirmations are instructions to remind ourselves of what we want our life to be like.

Our words and thoughts convey a tremendous amount of power and influence. Virtually everything we say or think to ourselves, either positive or negative, will come back to either help us as a friend or hurt us as an enemy. No matter what new belief or attitude we wish to implement, our minds cannot do so as long as our thoughts and comments continue to offer a negative counterpoint. The more we repeat affirmations, the more conviction and meaning we put into them, the more influence and power they will have over us.

Many of our affirmations are unconscious. We repeat words and phrases to ourselves (and to our children) out of pure habit rather than out of conscious choice. Without knowing it we may be delivering to ourselves and our children dozens of negative messages every day. We may not realize that these subconscious messages based on our words, are forming our view of ourselves and helping our children to form theirs.

Using affirmations can help your children gravitate toward greater happiness. It can help to eliminate any inconsistencies you have between what you really want for your children and the hidden messages you might currently be conveying. If your actual conversations with your children conflict with what you are hoping to teach them about being a happy person, you will be working against yourself and against your children.

Suppose, for example, that one of your goals for your child is to help her with her problem of "always being bored." If, when your child starts whining about being bored, you say to her: "You're always bored. What's wrong with you?" you will have reinforced to her how incapable she is of being creative. She may even interpret your comment as a suggestion that she is incapable of being happy. After all, you are a most important person in her life, someone she looks to for truth and guidance. If you say, "You're always bored" why would she question it? It may have felt good to get your feelings off your chest, and you may feel justified in "speaking the truth," but the negative affirmation—You're always bored—can become a self-fulfilling prophesy: the repetition of those words in her mind can encourage her to view herself in this way.

Learning about the power of both positive and negative affirmations can help you eliminate feedback from you that compounds your child's problems. I encourage and remind you to use only words and phrases that help your children. In the above example, you might have rephrased your affirmation to your child to something like: "I know that you are a happy and creative person. Give it some thought; I'm sure you'll think of something really fun to do." By using these more positive words, you will be giving your child the hidden message that you believe in her and her capacities absolutely. You have let your child know that you trust that she alone knows best what is best for her.

The Subconscious Mind

Positive and negative affirmations reflect your subconscious mind. This part of your mind is subconscious because it's not so available to your awareness—and it's not on the surface of your child's awareness either. This part of your mind controls your actions—and you may not be aware of it. Do you sometimes look back at something you did and say, "Was that really me that did that?" You are what your subconscious mind thinks you are, and you will act according to how your subconscious mind thinks you should act. It is critical that your child's subconscious be filled up with beliefs that testify that he or she is a very happy and capable person.

The subconscious mind is a sponge. It hears your words and thoughts—which define how you see yourself—and soaks them up. Because you, the parent, are so important to your children, always be aware of what you say to them. The simplest comments can be devastating to your children, particularly if they are said over and over again, day after day.

The subconscious mind has no judgment over what it hears and it does not understand jokes or humor. All it does is listen, so that it will know how to behave. Even seemingly harmless statements and nicknames register somewhere in your children's subconscious mind, and will affect how they view themselves and how they behave. A parent who nicknames his child "Mr. Boring" may be doing so only out of fun, but the child's subconscious mind understands only that he is called "Mr. Boring" and thinks he should act and feel accordingly. When he complains that there is "nothing to do," it should come as no surprise to the parent who has so named him.

Of course you are not solely responsible if your child is bored. But if a child is predisposed to boredom, try not to remind him of how bored he is. If he is in the habit of rushing around, don't call him "Mr. Hyper" even if he is hyper, even if the family thinks it's funny.

Use of affirmations will not deny any real issues your child is facing. You are not unaware of the facts or *pretending* that your child is not in the habit of being bored; you are attempting to reverse a tendency he has to think of himself in that negative way. Rather than reinforce to your child those negative beliefs that she has about herself, start up a new train of thought; this will eventually become the new way that she sees herself.

The subconscious mind has nothing else to do but wait for instructions. As far as your children are concerned, many of these "instructions" come from you. Consequently, it's important to minimize and eventually eliminate the number of times you verbalize any type of negative message to your children. Teach your children the same wisdom. Gently guide them to speak and think of themselves in ways that encourage only positive growth. Help them get into the habit of being kind and loving to themselves.

If children continue to hear and tell themselves negative things, they will begin to believe them. Take, for example, a child who says over and over, "I'm always nervous." The following process will occur in the subconscious mind:

▲ The words will register in the subconscious for processing.

▲ The mind will immediately recognize that it is giving attention to "nervousness."

▲ The subconscious is now focused on "nervousness," and begins to reinforce that this "way of being" (nervousness) is beyond control.

▲ You begin to believe it's just in your nature to be anxious or nervous, and there is nothing you can do about it. Your subconscious tells you that "nervousness" is part of your make-up as a human being.

Telling a "hyper" child that he is hyper simply reminds him or reinforces and accentuates the problem. Your intention may be positive (pure love for your child), but negative messages will only make matters worse.

The subconscious mind is absolutely consistent with its habits. If you and your children can change the emphasis of your statements from negative to positive, the subconscious will put an equal amount of effort into forming a positive view, validating your words.

If you happen to slip and use negative words or conversation around your children, forgive yourself. I've done it myself many times, as have we all. Maybe now that you understand the power that your words have on your children, you may find yourself respecting that power.

Focus attention on what you can do *now* to help your

child; forget what you have done in the past. Be always conscious of what you tell your child, from this point forward. Make a vow to strive toward the goal of never again giving your children unfair or unnecessary criticism, or hidden messages that will hurt their self-esteem.

Affirmations as a Tool

In addition to becoming more aware of what you say to your children, affirmations can be practiced as a form of positive thinking and reprogramming. If your children are old enough, you can teach them to repeat affirmations to themselves as a means of instilling a more positive self-image. The reason this can be an important tool for some children is that it can begin to override any negative beliefs they might have about themselves with more positive ones.

Ultimately, children respond to life according to how they view themselves. Children who think of themselves as confident will act confidently. Children who think of themselves as attractive will feel good about their appearance. In actuality, there is really no such thing as attractive; there is only how we think of ourselves. This is why two people with similar physical appearances may have drastically different views of themselves.

If we can change the way we think about ourselves, we might also begin to feel better about ourselves. How? Affirmations can be a stepping stone for ourselves and our children to get into the habit of speaking to ourselves more positively. If your child gets into the habit of speaking well of herself in this way, she will see herself as a well person; she will love herself and the world she lives in.

Affirmations to Share with Your Children

I love my life.
I'm so happy.
Things come easily to me.
I'm a relaxed person.
I'm gentle and loving.
I'm excited about life.
I love to create.
I have a great imagination.
I have nice friends.
I love people.
People love me.
Life is fun.
It's easy for me to relax.

Create your own list depending on the beliefs you want to help your children to change.

Tips to Make Affirmations Useful

▲ Affirmations are meant to be fun, easy, and light. Don't turn them into something your child "must do." Simply practice them, say them aloud, and encourage your child to practice them when it feels right.

▲ The shorter and simpler, the more effective. Affirmations should be clear, direct statements that convey a strong and positive feeling.

▲ Affirm what you want, not what you don't want. Affirmations will form a visual picture in your mind. The statement "I am not anxious" will likely promote a vision of an anxious person, whereas the affirmation

"I am very calm" brings up the visual image of a calm person.

▲ Phrase affirmations in the present tense, as if what you are affirming already exists. For example, "I am calm" works better than "Someday I will be calm."

▲ Enthusiasm is a key to success, and kids love enthusiasm. We are much more effective when we are enthusiastic about something. Being excited makes it easier and more fun to find a way to create success.

Repeat the message, "Life is fun to me." Say it like you mean it! Give this affirmation a try right now.

Life is fun to me!

The words have much more meaning and power when you say it like you mean it. And the same will be true for your children. Encourage your children to mean what they say and to practice their affirmations enthusiastically.

▲ Use repetition to reinforce the notion. The more your children repeat a positive message to themselves, the more they will impress upon their subconscious minds the valuable messages they are giving themselves.

Creating a Self-Talk Tape

Helping your children create a self-talk tape will encourage them to use affirmations efficiently and effectively. A tape of your voice (or their own, if they are old enough) practicing affirmations geared toward the goal of happiness can be a powerful tool for change. By listening to this tape, children hear over and over again the positive messages you want them to hear about themselves.

Ten Steps to a Creative Self-Talk Tape

(These are guidelines, not mandates.)

1. Purchase a 15- or 30-minute endless loop tape so the messages you create can continue repeating until you (or your child) decide to turn them off.

2. Create a specific list of affirmations that you want your child to hear. Arrange them in an order that makes sense to you.

3. Use your child's name in the statements. If your daughter's name is Mary, say, "I, Mary, love my life."

4. For maximum results, use present tense. Say "I am easygoing," rather than "I will be easygoing someday."

5. Use only positive words and phrases.

6. Get to the point. Be brief. If you want to convey the message that life is enjoyable, say "I love life" instead of "I love life when everything around me is going well and when I feel good."

7. Believe in your heart that what you are saying is the truth. Your belief in your children will come across on the tape.

8. The messages should sound positive and self-assured. Record them onto your tape as many times as you have to until they sound just the way your children will enjoy hearing them.

9. Avoid seriousness. This exercise is meant to be fun for your children.

10. Don't worry about doing it "right." That's not important. What is important is that you make the tape that's right for you, and for your child.

CHAPTER TEN

AVOIDING CRITICISM

Most children need more love than they deserve.

—ANONYMOUS

VERY FEW PARENTS CONSCIOUSLY SET OUT to hurt their children with criticism, so it's important to understand how criticism can drain the happiness right out of a youngster. Negative criticism is a waste of time; it only serves to squelch an otherwise happy person. Criticism is based on the following premises: "You're not good enough," "There are better ways to do things," "Why can't you do things my way?," "Don't trust your own instincts—trust mine instead" or, "Your decisions don't matter."

All forms of criticism, including so-called constructive criticism, lower a child's spirits and sense of self-worth and teach him to question himself and to distrust what he feels in his heart. Criticism hurts children—especially when it comes from their parents. You are your child's number one role model and he is your number one fan. Your child looks to you, to either verify or contradict what he already feels inside himself. Since children begin their life feeling good about themselves and their efforts, all you have to do is find creative ways to reinforce their natural belief systems. Go along with them; use plenty of encouragement and praise.

The need to dish out criticism stems from a bad habit of looking for what's wrong in life. It's a habit that is easy to fall into because everywhere you look you will find other people doing the same thing. If you've been engaged in the habit of criticism, don't be hard on yourself—you have lots of company. But just because everyone criticizes doesn't mean it's a good idea.

Your First Apartment as a Model

Think back to the time when you first moved out of your family home and into your own apartment. If this hasn't happened to you yet, see if you can recognize the pattern anyway.

You're on your own for the very first time. You move into a studio apartment barely the size of your old bedroom. You love it! You wouldn't change a thing. It's perfect—just the way it is. You think you could be happy here forever.

A few months down the road you wake up one morning and notice that you don't like the color of the walls. You get the idea to paint the apartment. Once you are finished, you notice that the blinds aren't quite right either. You go downtown to pick out some new ones. Shortly after you install your new blinds, you notice your art hanging on the wall is ugly. Next it's the bedding, then the woodwork, then the trim, the carpet, and on and on and on you go.

It isn't wrong or inappropriate to alter or decorate your physical surroundings. But it is a strong human tendency to get into a mental habit of "looking for what's wrong." This habit starts out innocently and often the stakes are small. A little improvement here, a little more there, and so on. But pretty soon it can become a habit, a way of life that begins to take over your thinking process. The result of this habit is dissatisfaction and distress. The same things that used to bring you joy now look like eyesores.

The same habit of looking for what's wrong with your children can take hold if you aren't careful. A little suggestion here, another one there can lead to an overabundance of criticism. Virtually all children eventually feel that their parents dish out too much criticism. Is it any wonder why so many children lose their inherent happiness?

A point to keep in mind is that all people—children too—learn better, and are more open to suggestion and change when they feel good about themselves. A little less criticism on your part will be followed by a little more cooperation on your child's part. A lot less criticism will lead to a lot more cooperation.

Guidance Versus Criticism

You might confuse a lack of criticism with a lack of loving guidance, that criticism is the only way to show your children to the correct path. But criticism is only one form of guidance, negative guidance based on a deficiency model of living. In a sense, the criticism model of guidance says: Tell your child enough that he isn't good enough and he will come around to the "right way."

Loving guidance is quite different. It is based on a model of growth. Guidance is based on the premise that your child is perfect just the way he is—right now. If he didn't change one inch, if he never learned to crawl, or to walk, or to read,

71

or to do his math problems, it shouldn't matter to you. Of course, you want these things for your child but you mustn't require them in exchange for your love. You would love him just as much—forever—if he never changed one bit.

The guidance model goes on to say: Given the fact that your child is perfect—and he knows in his heart that he is perfect and also knows that you feel he is perfect—go ahead and encourage him to improve himself, to be the very best that he can. The guidance model works well in parenting, because children love to learn and excel when they don't feel pressured, when they feel that it's okay to be a beginner and to make mistakes.

People who don't feel good about themselves, or who don't feel as though it's okay to make mistakes, feel threatened when they think about improving. So, if you say to your child who doesn't feel very good about himself, "You don't work very hard on your math, it's no wonder you do so poorly," you are reinforcing an already negative self-outlook. A likely response is going to be "Who cares anyway?"

Children who are approached with guidance instead of criticism feel they have nothing to lose when you offer a suggestion. A parent who says, "I know you have it in you to do well in math and I have confidence that you can do it. Let's see if we can work together to improve your skills," is instilling a vote of confidence into their child's mind. With self-assurance, children can do just about anything.

Nothing to Lose

Think how much fun it would be to gamble with "risk capital," money that you don't mind losing! This is different from gambling with your grocery money. Growth and self-improvement work in a similar fashion. If you approach growth from a guidance perspective, your child has nothing to lose; in a sense he has already won the game; he already has your approval, and now he is only playing for fun. But if you approach growth and improvement from a criticism perspective, you are playing with your child's "grocery money"—he is going to feel that he has *everything* to lose. If he can't do something to your expectation and satisfaction, he will feel like a failure. And because he feels so insecure, he is more likely to fail.

"I Wouldn't Do That If I Were You"

How many times have you heard this statement in your life? How many times have you said it to others? Of course you wouldn't do it the way someone else would. Neither would anyone else. You are unique and special and so are your children. Everyone sees life differently and their behavior and actions will demonstrate this difference. Your child couldn't do something exactly the same way that you would do it, anymore than you could imitate the actions of the family dog. Every time you make this statement to your child, you suggest that he isn't as good as you, that his decisions aren't good the way he has made them, that he needs your approval, and he needs you to tell him how to run his life. Remember the hidden messages!

This pattern can begin early on with your children. For example, many parents will redress their toddler right after the little guy has just proudly picked out and put on his choice of an outfit. I know it can be hard to swallow when your child puts on a green-striped nightshirt with pink and

73

blue unmatching socks and purple pants; believe me, it's happened to me too. But what kind of message do you want to convey to your youngster? Is it more important that he is dressed to perfection for the grocery store clerk to admire, or that he feel proud, self-confident, and happy about his own wonderful efforts?

Criticizing your children less is as easy as making a commitment to do so. *Most criticism is nothing more than a habit that has become a way of life, a mind-set.* If you decide to stop criticizing your children, you can and will stop doing it! When you are aware of the negative effect that criticism has on your children you will stop. Your children will notice, and they will be grateful to you for the rest of their lives! Your children want you to love them just the way they are—not the way they could be, or should be, or might be, but just the way they already are.

CHAPTER ELEVEN

TAKING RISKS

Heroism feels and never reasons and therefore is always right.
—RALPH WALDO EMERSON

OR YOUR CHILDREN TO LIVE UP to their full potential, and grow into self-confident, happy adults, encourage a healthy attitude toward risk-taking. All happy people take at least some regular risks in their life—not crazy or dangerous risks, but reasonable risks likely to expand their experience and make life more rewarding.

Risk-taking is a step into the unknown, an affirmation to yourself that it's okay not to know what is going to happen next. A child who is lovingly encouraged to take risks will likely grow up with a creative attitude, willing to try new things, travel to new places, meet new people, and participate in new activities. Risk-takers are leaders in their fields who come up with new ideas. They are innovators who break traditions that no longer work, and they are not afraid to speak their mind. Risk-takers are willing to stand up for what they feel is right, even if it goes against popular opinion. If someone is being mistreated by the crowd, a risk-taker is invariably the one who comes to his rescue.

The opposite of risk-taking is "playing it safe," always knowing the logical conclusion of every action before you take it. Children who are not allowed to take risks often grow up to be frightened by novel things, adventures, unfamiliar places and people. Non-risk-takers almost always choose to do things "the way it's always been done," the safe way, the "right" way. They prefer predictability over adventure, even if they don't really like that which is predictable. Feeling safe is seen, on an internal level, as more important than feeling fulfilled.

Risk-taking is a natural, ever-exhilarating process that is already built in to the human psyche. Without the innate desire to take risks, none of us would ever learn to walk or talk. If we were discouraged at our earliest efforts to try these basic activities, we would quickly become extinct as a species. Risk-taking is an important part of a full and happy life. Although it's hard to watch your children stumble and fall, it is nevertheless an important part of their development—to enable them to walk and talk, and as an overall attitude toward life. Children who learn that it's not okay to take risks, who are discouraged from stepping into the unknown, often live an empty, mechanical life filled exclusively with "safe" activities.

Being a Beginner

Risk-takers feel intuitively that it's okay to be a beginner. They know that there is nothing wrong with learning something new, from starting at the beginning, from being the least advanced person in a class. Risk-takers do not think of themselves, or others, as foolish when they are learning something new. They never berate themselves with criticism because they aren't an expert on their first attempts at something—and they give the same respect to others. Risk-takers never laugh at someone for trying, even if that person has very little apparent skill. They applaud beginners. They know it takes far more courage to be the worst in the class than it does to be the best.

A beginner's mind is a creative mind—a creative mind is a happy mind. A happy person is willing to say, "I don't know, but I will try." A creative, happy person has an adventuresome spirit willing to try practically anything. Although willing to try new things, a creative person is unlikely to experiment with dangerous things such as drugs and violence. The reason: A happy, creative person turns inside to her own wisdom for answers. She isn't a sheep who follows the herd. She never does anything just because everyone else is doing it. A creative, happy person doesn't need external "highs" because life is rich and rewarding without them.

An expert's mind doesn't see anything new. An "expert" is merely reviewing what he already knows. Often, doing something the same, expert way it has been done before *is* creative. For example, an Olympic gymnast may practice the same program ten thousand times in exactly the same way. That skill is creative, to be cultivated. The difference lies in the *attitude* of the doer, the degree of openness to change. A creative person may in fact opt to do something in "the same old way," but she isn't "locked-in" to doing so. The gymnast who feels the routine getting stale will modify it, or create a new one, in order to take fresh risks.

77

Going Beyond Your "Comfort Zone"

Creative people have a wide-arcing learning curve because they are constantly moving beyond the "comfort zone." A comfort zone is simply your normal or usual way of doing something. For example, a teenager may love writing, and his comfort zone may include writing everything long-hand with a pen or pencil. One day someone offers him a computer so he can learn to use a word processor as a tool. A creative person would probably say, "Thank you, I'd love to give it a try." He would be open-minded, willing to see whether or not the use of a computer could help him work toward writing out his dreams. He may or may not decide to continue using the computer—but he would certainly be willing to try it.

An uncreative person might decline the offer altogether because he's never typed before. He would be unwilling to venture into the unknown because he is unaccustomed to taking risks. To him, it is never okay to be a beginner. So he would miss out on wonderful opportunities—which might have expanded his horizons in ways he never knew were possible.

Going beyond your comfort zone means a willingness to take small risks—even if you fail. Rely on the self-confidence that is generated from a lifetime commitment to growth and learning. Risk-takers know that some failure is inevitable; they also know that success and satisfaction in life come from a willingness to take risks.

Courage

My father taught me that courage is not doing something in the absence of fear—it is doing something even though you are fearful. If a child isn't frightened to travel to the mountains with his friends, she isn't demonstrating courage by going along. If she is frightened and decides to do it anyway, then she is exhibiting tremendous courage.

If you ask top athletes or musicians whether or not they get nervous before a performance, most will tell you that they do. If you ask public speakers whether or not they feel butterflies before giving a lecture, many of them will say, "Of course I do." Great people know that it's okay to be afraid—it can even be fun and usually leads to a feeling of satisfaction after the challenge is met. Risk-takers know that a wonderful feeling of exhilaration results from doing something that you are afraid to do.

Remember how nervous you used to be before calling (or receiving a call from) your sweetheart in junior high school? You were nervous, but it was fun! How rewarding would it have felt if you felt no trembling at all—no emotion? It would have felt empty.

Teach your children that it's okay to be scared; it's okay to take something on, even though you are frightened. Creativity takes courage—courage to face an uncertain outcome or the critical opinions of others. Creative people are not free from fear, they have an attitude of "Oh well, I'll give it a try."

Regrets Result
from Unattempted Challenges

In my entire adult lifetime, I've met very few people who regretted things they tried that were unsuccessful. Almost always, regret is tied to a life that wasn't fully lived, activities never attempted, career changes that never happened, places never visited, people never met, and so forth.

As we look back at our life, we have a profound understanding that failure is nothing to be afraid of; it is a necessary component to life, which helps shape our direction. We learn and grow from every failure. No one likes it, but it has to happen.

Creative children grow up to have almost no regrets because they were willing to take chances and follow their own path. Fostering a creative, risk-taking attitude in your child is a gift that will ensure a happy, adventuresome life.

Five Simple Ways to Encourage Risk-Taking

1. Take a class with your child on something you know nothing about.

Take a ballet class or a model-building class, something different—something you know nothing about. Be the only man in an all-women's class, or the only woman in an all-men's class. Show your children that it's okay to be different and it's okay to be a beginner.

2. Praise people for trying.

Never say "Look at that fool." Never laugh at someone because he isn't an expert. If you do, your child will learn to avoid new things for fear of looking like a fool. Instead, praise people for trying new things. Applaud beginners. Give them as much, or more, praise than the winner.

3. Ask your child what he would like to do that he's never done before.

Rather than repeating last week's activities, ask your child to think of something he's always wanted to do. If he can't think of anything, participate in the exercise. "Let's see, I wonder if it would be fun to. . . . " Encourage newness and exploration.

4. Encourage enthusiasm for the unknown.

Whenever your child says, "I wonder what it would be like to try . . . ," encourage it. Respond with an enthusiastic, "I'm sure you can." If possible, try it too. Say, "Hey, maybe we could check it out together."

5. Be willing to undertake some discomfort or inconvenience to help your child experience newness.

If your child decides it would be interesting to get up at 5 A.M. to watch the sun rise, or wants to start a jogging program early in the morning, ask permission, then go along. Demonstrate that newness is worth the effort. If your child is frightened to try something new, offer to do it too, saying "We'll never know what's it's like until we try."

CHAPTER TWELVE

BOREDOM

Boredom is caused by a busy mind.

—RICHARD CARLSON

B OREDOM IS ONE OF THE TRICKIEST AREAS for parents to deal with because it appears to be something that it is not. Boredom has nothing whatsoever to do with not having enough to do, and everything to do with having an overactive, busy mind. Boredom is an important topic to understand because so many children complain of it. Without a clear understanding of where boredom stems from, you can inadvertently create *more* boredom in your children.

Think back to the last time you sat in front of a beautiful roaring fire with someone you love. You sat for hours, contented, absorbed in each special moment. You are not "doing much," your mind is clear and free, you are in a healthy thought process—you are anything but bored. Whenever you are in this healthy, present-moment-oriented thought process you feel satisfied; life is "just right."

Now think back to the last time you were stuck in traffic. You may have been caught for only a few minutes, yet you were probably bored stiff—right? There was enough "going on" around you to prevent you from getting bored, certainly *far more* than there was in front of some fireplace. Yet, boredom sets in, in a matter of minutes.

Why? Because as you sit in traffic your mind begins to rush around to all the places you'd rather be and all the things you'd rather be doing. Rather than sitting quietly and experiencing the moment (as you would do in your healthy thought process), your thinking mind plunges toward the future (How am I going to get out of this?) or backward to the past (How did I get myself into this?). You allow your mind to "speed up" and "fill up" to the point of an "unhealthy thought process." The busier your mind gets, the further you move away from the present moment, and the less satisfaction you feel.

In front of the fireplace, your mind was relatively free from distraction. Your thoughts were flowing, and your mind was clear. Because there wasn't an overabundance (too much) of thought in your head, you were able to enjoy something as simple as a roaring fire. As your head fills up with excess thoughts, however, your ability to enjoy the moment is removed. This dynamic will happen wherever you are. As your mind gets filled with concerns and worries, you become less able to enjoy yourself, your children, or even a vacation.

The next time you feel bored, or the next time your child says she feels bored, take a look (or get a sense from your child) at the quantity of thought, or level of mental activity, in your (or your child's) head. The more overactive the mind is, the less able you will be to enjoy your life. This dynamic is always true. Your child could be in the most beautiful place on earth, but if her mind is overactive, she won't be able to see the beauty. She will be too "busy" evaluating what she is seeing, or she will be thinking about something else.

Most people think boredom comes from not having anything (enough things) to do. So when they feel bored, they look elsewhere, for something else. Because it takes so much stimulus to satisfy a person with a "busy mind," the only answer seems to be to look for more stimulus. This cycle becomes a way of life. Schedules get filled up in an attempt to feel satisfied and contented.

The implications of this to you, as a parent, are important. If your child says to you: "Mom, I'm bored," it suggests that your child has an overactive, busy mind, not a lack of things to do. If his mind were calm, slowed down, if he were more "present," it wouldn't matter what he was doing—he would enjoy it. This doesn't suggest that he wouldn't want or need diverse activities in his life, or that he shouldn't have preferences; it means that he wouldn't feel bored. If he were absorbed in the activities that he *was* doing, rather than thinking about what else he could be doing, in a more present-moment-oriented state of mind, the smallest experiences would feel rich and rewarding. When your child says, "Mom, I'm bored," don't jump, drop what you are doing, and create something for the child to do. Doing so will only "fuel the fire," giving the overactive mind even more to think about. An already busy mind will get even busier, and your child's ability to feel satisfied will grow further out of reach.

A better solution is to say something like, "It's okay to be bored. Just relax for a few minutes and something will occur to you." Here, you are giving the hidden (but direct) message to clear the mind and relax. As the overabundance of thought diminishes something creative will pop up. Instead of being bored, your child will sit back, relax, and experience and enjoy life in the present moment.

When you see the signs of a busy mind (boredom setting in), keep in mind what is *really* causing the boredom—a busy mind, not lack of activity. Gently suggest to your child, "Relax, when your mind quiets down, your wisdom will tell you what to do next."

What do you suppose would happen to your positive experience of sitting in front of the fire if your mind started worrying about something? Within a matter of seconds, you would be wishing you were somewhere else, doing something different. Satisfaction would disappear. Your mind would be so busy, you would feel you needed things to do, that "something else," taking action, would bring you greater satisfaction. Once you changed positions though, your mind would start the process all over again. A never-ending cycle of dissatisfaction begins, where your mind keeps telling you, "something else" will bring you joy.

The solution to boredom is to stay more in the present moment. When a child's mind (or an adult's) is not overly busy, immersed in the present moment, boredom doesn't exist. You could be "as busy as a bee" or just "hanging out," doing nothing. The activity isn't relevant, in fact makes no difference at all. What is relevant is the child's state of mind, a willingness to be comfortable when there is little going on.

Waiting for Something to Happen

Happy people (children and adults) have moments when nothing is on their minds. They welcome these moments, because they open the door for inspiration. Happy people use these quiet moments to access wisdom and creativity—a vehicle to tell them what to do next. Happy children know intuitively that creativity is a process that bubbles up inside them automatically when their mind is clear and quiet—they don't have to "figure out" what to do next—something will just occur to them.

A person who frequently experiences boredom might think of a quiet mind as "boring." The very thought of having nothing to do causes panic, so he quickly creates something to replace the quiet. Consequently, his mind is almost never quiet. To him, anything is better than "nothing." His goal, whether conscious or unconscious, is to fill every moment of his life with some kind of activity. How many of us can sit, even for two minutes, without doing something or thinking actively about something? Very few. This is important, because those moments when your mind is free of distraction are the very moments when you have the greatest potential for creativity. The same is true for your child. If he can learn to appreciate and trust that his quiet moments can serve him, his creative potential will soar.

Children need permission from you to relax and do nothing. Some parents become almost immobilized if their children have even a few minutes a day when nothing is going on. "They're not being productive," is a common fear. You can rest assured that if your children can learn to relax, if they can have moments during the day when everything is quiet, when nothing is going on, they will be plenty productive. When they do make a decision, it will be made from a place of wisdom and not from a place of panic or fear. They won't be "killing time."

I've talked in public lectures about this inability to sit still and I am frequently asked: "Wouldn't my child become a bump on the log if she learned to sit still?" Hardly. I'm talking about a few minutes a day—perhaps ten to twenty out of the 1440 that are available to us—to simply appreciate a quiet mind. Your child won't be a bump on a log but rather a creative and happy genius.

The willingness to have a clear or empty mind ensures that your child will never again experience boredom. When she learns to welcome those infrequent moments when nothing much is on her mind, she increases the awe and wonder in her life: the smallest things will again bring her joy. She will begin to see aspects of her life that were previously invisible because her mind won't be so filled up with the old; instead it will be receptive to newness.

When your child's mind is spinning, or working hard, it is constantly reviewing that which it already knows. Her busy mind is filled with comparisons, interpretations of whatever is going on, what has happened before. Her mind gets too busy to notice the beauty of life, to enjoy childhood. If the mind never quiets down during the day, life gets eaten up with wanting more and more and more. This, to me, is truly boring!

Grazing

A helpful analogy for those trying to understand the essence of a "quiet mind" is to think of horses grazing in a field. Horses wander around looking for food—they don't focus on any one area for very long. They let themselves drift from place to place.

So too with a quiet mind. It doesn't focus on any one thought for long. Thoughts come, then they flow out. Not much attention is given to any single thought. They are all treated equally. A quiet mind is a mind at rest, an animal "grazing" in a field.

In your child's quiet moments, she will have frequent inspirations, insights that will delight and surprise you. Thoughts like "*That's* what I need to do" or "That's so obvious." No matter what age, your child will find new solutions to important questions.

Just the other day my oldest daughter and I turned on soft music and sat quietly together. I cleared my mind the best that I was able to, and it seemed as if she did too. After about ten minutes of sitting quietly together, we decided to drive to the local reservoir to rent a paddle boat. The benefit we both received from our quiet time together was immense. First, we were able to enjoy each other's company for some time without "doing" much. Then we relaxed together for the rest of the afternoon, and appreciated one another.

Before I understood the value of a quiet mind I can honestly say that I might have experienced our time together listening to music as boring. After all, we weren't "doing" anything! Instead of loving every second of our quiet time together, and enjoying my time with my daughter, I would have been struggling to come up with something to do. I wouldn't have realized that we were doing exactly what we needed to be doing. And I'm certain that I wouldn't have come up with anything as creative as renting a boat together. I have learned that when my mind is quiet my creativity is enhanced. The same is true with my children.

Teach Your Children to Enjoy Quiet Moments

Teaching your children to enjoy rather than struggle with their quiet moments requires nothing more than an example from you that it's okay to not be doing something. Your chil-

89

dren need your permission to appreciate a quiet mind. We live in such a "doing" world that often children feel they should be busy every second of every day.

I'm not talking about very much time here, maybe only a few minutes a day. The critical message you want to get across is that a quiet mind is not to be feared, but is something to welcome and embrace. When the mind is clear, it opens the door for new and creative ideas, things that will be fun. It will take very few times for your children to see that this is true. Whenever their mind gets clear, a good idea will follow. In time, your children will be leading delightful lives filled with inspiration and newness!

Five Tendencies That Promote Boredom in Children

1. *Filling every moment with something to do.*

If you never have empty moments when nothing is going on in your household, your child will learn to cram too much into life; her mind will be too busy to enjoy life and she will get what she least wants—boredom! Planning too many activities during the course of a day or a week takes the spontaneity and joy out of the activities. It leaves no space to take a breath or to reflect on what you have done. It instills the belief of more, more, more.

2. *Acting bored yourself.*

Not being able to sit still yourself for a few minutes reinforces the notion that one must be doing something *all the time,* and that life is an emergency. This puts pressure on youngsters because it leaves no space to simply "be." Show your children how fun and easy it is to relax and have nothing to do. Being bored is one of the most common complaints we hear from our children. It can be conquered with your help.

3. *Upping the ante.*

Parents whose goal is to outdo last year's vacation or have more fun than last time may only be doing so to encourage good times—but they are actually encouraging boredom. Children who grow up in these families develop a tendency to compare everything and think "more is better." Rather than enjoying experiences for the sake of enjoyment, they decide in advance if they will enjoy something, based on a previous experience. Even if today's activity turns out to be as much fun as last time, these children lose out because they are already wondering if "next time" will be as much fun. The problem stems from an overactive mind. Encourage your children to enjoy each experience as it happens—not to think so much about it.

4. *Confusing excitement with exhilaration.*

Exhilaration is a natural high that is created through your own imagination and creativity. It feels great and never leaves you disappointed or bored. Excitement, on the other hand, is made. There is nothing wrong with excitement, but too much can be overstimulating and lead to boredom. Children who get too much excitement (too many trips to Disneyland, too many movies, too much television, too many computer games) can come to rely on it. Encourage natural exhilaration over artificial excitement and your children will never be disappointed.

5. *Giving too many toys.*

Don't shower your children with too many toys. The hidden message is: You need these things to make you happy. You are incapable of entertaining yourself! Strive to strike a thoughtful balance.

▲ ▲ ▲

If your children experience boredom, it isn't your fault— but you can take steps to reduce it. Boredom is learned—it isn't inherent. If you stop acting bored yourself, if you stop panicking at the first sign of quiet, and you stop participating in actions that promote boredom, your household will be "boredom-free" before you know it.

Boredom is caused by a busy mind. If you learn to quiet down, and teach your children to do the same, your life together will reach a new level of joy. Instead of fear, quiet moments will cause rejuvenation and delight in you and your children. Quiet times will become an ongoing source of inspiration and wisdom.

CHAPTER THIRTEEN

CULTIVATING A GRATEFUL ATTITUDE

One chief idea of my life . . . is the idea of taking things with gratitude and not taking things for granted.

—G. K. CHESTERTON

DO YOU EVER SAY: "WHY AREN'T MY CHILDREN more grateful for all that I do for them?" Perhaps the best place to find an answer is to examine your own stance toward gratitude. Is gratitude something that you practice only every once in a while, before dinner, or on Sundays? Or is gratitude an attitude you have toward life, something as natural to you as riding a bike? How often do you say, in front of your children, "I'm so grateful for your presence in my life. I'm so happy to be alive."

Great thinkers and wise people throughout history have encouraged us to be grateful for what we have. The rationale behind this wisdom is simple. Gratitude feels good! Gratitude is a feeling that bubbles up inside, bringing out the best we have to offer, both to ourselves and to others. A grateful attitude directs our attention toward what we have—instead of what we are lacking. When we are grateful it dictates our entire experience of life, making it rich, satisfying, and fulfilling.

Your mind (and your child's mind) is like a magnet. It gravitates toward what you think about the most. If you focus on feeling grateful for what you have, those thoughts will grow, and you will get more of the same, only better. And, when your attention is focused on what you lack, what is missing from your life, you will continue to attract emptiness because this is where your attention lies. The irony of this is that the more you focus on what you have, instead of what you don't have, the less you end up wanting. And the less you want, the more you get! Really!

People who live the most fulfilling lives rejoice in what they already have—and the people who live the least joyful lives are constantly complaining about what they don't have. In both cases, the irrelevant factor is what you actually have; the relevant factor is where you place your attention. If you concentrate on the good in your partner, that is what you will see; if you concentrate on the positive qualities in your children, you will enjoy their presence in your life. But the reverse is also true. You might have the most wonderful, playful child in the world, but if your attention is on the one little negative quirk in his personality, then your experience of your child will be that quirk. You will sabotage your own enjoyment of your child because of your belief that things could be better if that quirk weren't there. The quirk isn't the problem, but that you are focusing on it! If the quirk or problem disappeared, your attention would probably seek out yet another imperfection.

All this negativity is simply a bad habit. It can be changed by understanding the dynamic at work and making the commitment to change it. We all practice this bad habit at times, focusing on one or two negative things that aren't working instead of marvelling at how much does work. How many things has your child managed not to lose? How often is your child on time? How many questions did your child answer correctly on an exam? These are the right questions to be asking. Focusing on "what's wrong" never helps a child; it only hurts. Starting right now, begin looking for "what's right" with your life, and what's right with your children. Practice doing this even when you don't feel like it and you will quickly find yourself enjoying yourself and your children as you never have before.

Try this new attitude of gratefulness today and watch your experience as a parent change before your eyes. Instead of focusing on what's wrong with your children, you'll put your attention on what's right and beautiful. You'll feel grateful and happy. Practice being where you are, look at what you have instead of what you don't have. As you do, you will see that you have far more to be grateful for than you ever thought. Your positive attitude will feed on itself and become an ongoing virtuous cycle. This new cycle will start with your intention to "see the good."

Gratitude is an attitude toward life. It has nothing whatsoever to do with how much you actually have or the circumstances in your life. If it did, then the more you had, the happier you would be. But this is not always true. We all know there are many unhappy, bored "spoiled brats," both children as well as adults, who appear to have everything they could ever want. There are also a few shining individuals who appear to have nothing at all, but act as though they have everything they could ever want. The difference between these people is that they've cultivated the habit of gratitude.

Optimism Versus Pessimism

There once was a story of two young brothers who were as different as two people could be. Jack was an unhappy pessimist who thought the world was out to get him. He didn't like anything, nothing could please him. Jack could find fault with anything and everything, and often did. His attitude toward life left him constantly dissatisfied. He spent most of the time complaining.

Jim was the opposite. He was happy, joyful, funny, and carefree. Full of wonderment and awe. Every morning when he woke up, he felt lucky to be alive. He almost always saw the good in everything and everyone. Jim was satisfied. He made the best of everything, wherever he was, and whomever he was with.

The parents of Jack and Jim were concerned about Jack's well-being, so they went to a psychiatrist for professional advice. "The solution is simple," he said. "Obviously Jack feels as though you treat Jim better than you treat him. Christmas is coming soon. Load Jack up with presents. Mortgage your home if you have to, but give him everything he could possibly want. And when it comes to Jim, don't give him a thing. In fact, fill up his room with something distasteful such as horse manure so that he will feel the way Jack has always felt. I know it sounds harsh, but you really need to even out the attention. It's the best thing for Jack."

As cruel as it sounded, the parents decided to take the good doctor's advice. On Christmas eve they filled up Jack's room with all the latest toys. They gave him everything a young child could possibly want. In Jim's room, they dumped a large load of horse manure. They filled it almost all the way to the ceiling just as the doctor had suggested.

When morning arrived, the parents ran into Jack's room to see the result of their efforts. But much to their surprise, Jack was moping. He wasn't one bit happier than he had been before. He was criticizing every toy, breaking them and throwing things, making comments like: "This isn't nearly as nice as some others I've seen."

Frustrated and confused, the parents turned their attention to Jim. "Maybe when Jack sees how upset Jim is, it will help him snap out of it," they thought. But when they opened Jim's door they were shocked! Jim was on top of the pile throwing the horse manure around and yelling, "Yipee, this is great. Thanks so much, Mom and Dad. I love it." "But Jim," they sang out together, "Why are you so happy? All you received was a big pile of horse manure!" Jim's reply: "You can't fool me—with all this manure all over the place there's bound to be a pony in here somewhere."

This funny story offers a powerful lesson to us all. It's our attitude toward life that makes us happy. You can decide to enjoy and be grateful, or you can decide that things must get better before you can be happy. The outcome has nothing to do with anything other than your attitude. Set a good example for your child. Help your child cultivate an attitude of gratefulness, and he or she will be among the happiest people on earth, and very grateful to *you*.

A Well-Kept Secret

One of the best-kept, yet easiest-to-understand secrets of happiness is: *To live a happy life, stay in the present moment—and be grateful in that moment for what you have!* That's it! Think about it. Whenever you can be totally absorbed in what you are doing, that activity is a potential source of joy. If you add a feeling of gratitude to that moment, your experience will be fulfilling, rewarding, rich, and full—it has to be. Even something as banal as washing dishes can be a rich experience, if you do it without also thinking about how often you have to do them, how many more there are to do, how much you wish you didn't have to do them, and so forth. If you simply wash the dishes, feel the water, keep your mind on what you are doing and feel grateful that you have dishes to wash, a home to wash them in, and beautiful children to feed, your experience of doing it will change.

Take a look at the types of things your children have fun doing: collecting rocks, running back and forth between random points, talking and singing to themselves, looking at leaves or graffiti. Anything can be a wonder, anything can be fun. What takes the fun *out* of an activity isn't the activity itself, but the attitude you have toward that activity. If you teach your child to think that collecting rocks is a waste of time, he will probably begin to think that you are right. He will take this attitude through his childhood and come to believe that all of life should be serious, and that little things like collecting rocks aren't important.

You can remind your children to be grateful by being more grateful yourself. Get down on the ground with them and agree with them about how terrific that leaf really is. Tell them every day how wonderful they are and how much you appreciate them. Let them know how grateful you are that you have them in your life, that you even have a life at all. Your example will rub off on your children. Gratitude is a natural feeling, and your children will be reminded of something they already intuitively know.

A Teaching Trick

Raising happy, creative, productive, high-achieving children has a lot to do with your ability to see the good in them. It's an irony, because it often seems more appropriate to point out what your child is doing wrong. You see her making or repeating a mistake and say: "You're always late, Sarah." The problem with this way of relating to your daughter is that it encourages Sarah to think of herself as a "person who is always late." If she sees herself this way, guess what? She will always be late. And while it can certainly be frustrating if your child is habitually late, it's more important to encourage your child to see herself as someone who is "on time." Look for opportunities and take advantage of them; everyone is on time once in a while. When she is, point it out. "Great, Sarah, on time again! It's amazing how often you are on time these days."

The same logic applies to boredom, scholarship, sports performance, and everything else. For a person to go through life confidently, he must first see himself in a positive light. In fact, it's impossible to be really good at anything if he thinks of himself as unqualified or "no good." And it's impossible to be happy if he thinks of himself as "unhappy." As parents, one of our jobs is to help our children see themselves as "good." The more we are able to do this, the easier it will be for our children to live happy, productive lives.

All people have an innate desire to improve themselves. No one wants to be a failure. For this reason, you can rest assured that it won't hurt your children if you fail to point it out to them every time they do something wrong. Occasionally, if a child needs the guidance, fine, but for the most part, focus more on the positive.

Gratitude and Satisfaction

Gratitude and satisfaction go hand in hand. The more gratitude a person feels, the more satisfied—the less grateful, the less satisfied. Cultivate a grateful attitude; without it, you really do have nothing. You can have everything in the world—possessions, relationships, health—but without appreciation for what you have, you won't feel you have anything. You will always be searching for something else, and forget to smell the roses right where you are and enjoy your life. Gratitude is the antidote for all dissatisfaction, and brings wonder and awe back to life.

Four Strategies
for Developing a Grateful Attitude

1. Stop complaining!

Everyone complains—but take a look at how much good it does. Zero! Complaining only makes you feel worse and it demonstrates to your children an ungrateful attitude, that you are more interested in what's wrong than in what's right. The moment you decide to stop complaining you will immediately improve the quality of your life.

2. Feel the difference between "low road" and "high road" thinking.

High road thinking feels good; it is grateful, appreciative, and has to do with what's right with your life. High road thinking brings the conversation up, and reminds everyone in the room how wonderful and special life really is. Low road thinking is all about what you need, what you don't have, dissatisfaction, things that bother you, and so on. Begin to notice when you are taking the "low road" and say to yourself, "Whoops, there I go again—forgetting how lucky I am."

3. Participate in service work with your children.

Demonstrate to your children that you care about people. Show them that there is more to life than themselves. Service work is something you can do together with your children. Most major cities have a volunteer center where you can learn more about service work—with the homeless, the hungry, the elderly, and the sick, to name just a few. These agencies love it when children become involved and they will usually teach your children what they can do to help. Children who learn, very early on, to help other people, feel very grateful for what they have. They develop compassion and kindness on a deep, personal level.

4. Make gratitude an integral part of everyday life.

Practice being thankful for anything and everything in your life. When you feel happy, let your children know it. Tell your children how grateful you are for them and for your life.

Additional Resources

For a list of books, tapes, and practitioners teaching healthy psychological functioning, send a written request along with a stamped, self-addressed envelope to:

Richard Carlson, Ph.D.
P.O. Box 1196
Orinda, CA 94563

About the Author

Dr. Richard Carlson is a nationally known stress management consultant practicing in Walnut Creek, California, where he teaches children and adults to live happier lives. He is the author of numerous books, including *You Can Be Happy No Matter What*. Dr. Carlson lives in Martinez, California, with his wife and two daughters.

Also by Dr. Richard Carlson

Healers on Healing (with Benjamin Shield), Tarcher, 1989

For the Love of God (with Benjamin Shield), New World Library, 1990

Everything I Eat Makes Me Thin (with Barbara Carlson), Bantam, 1991

You Can Be Happy No Matter What, New World Library, 1992

New World Library is dedicated to publishing books and cassettes that help improve the quality of our lives.

For a catalog of our fine books and cassettes, contact:

New World Library
58 Paul Drive
San Rafael, CA 94903
Phone: (415) 472-2100
FAX: (415) 472-6131

Or call toll free:

(800) 227-3900
In Calif.: (800) 632-2122